PRESS HERE!

REFLEXOLOGY

~ FOR BEGINNERS ~

PRESS HERE!

REFLEXOLOGY

~ FOR BEGINNERS ~

FOOT REFLEXOLOGY: A PRACTICE FOR PROMOTING HEALTH

STEFANIE SABOUNCHIAN

NB
NEW BURLINGTON

A QUARTO BOOK

First published in 2017 by
New Burlington Press
The Old Brewery
6 Blundell Street
London N7 9BH

QUAR.RFXF

ISBN: 978-0-85762-603-5

10 9 8 7 6 5 4 3 2 1

Digital edition published in 2017

Conceived, designed, and produced by
Quarto Publishing plc.
6 Blundell Street
London N7 9BH

Editor: Kate Burkett
Senior art editor: Emma Clayton
Designer and Illustrator: Emily Portnoi
Art director: Caroline Guest
Creative director: Moira Clinch
Publisher: Samantha Warrington

Printed in China

The information in this book is for educational purposes only. It is not intended to replace the advice of a physician or medical practitioner. Please see your health-care provider before beginning any new health program.

FSC
www.fsc.org
MIX
Paper from responsible sources
FSC® C016973

Contents

Chapter 3

WELCOME

MY FIRST INTRODUCTION TO THE ART AND SCIENCE OF REFLEXOLOGY WAS IN THE LATE 80S IN GERMANY, WHEN I ATTENDED A FOUR-DAY CLASS ON FOOT REFLEXOLOGY. WORKING AS A MEDICAL ASSISTANT AT THAT TIME, I WAS FASCINATED WITH THIS SIMPLE AND NON-INVASIVE WAY TO HELP PEOPLE HAVE LESS NECK OR BACK PAIN, SEE HEADACHES REDUCE WITHIN MINUTES AND TO HELP THEM JUST FEEL BETTER OVERALL – ALL THIS BY APPLYING UNIQUE THUMB AND FINGER TECHNIQUES ON A REFLEX MAP ON THE FEET!

I FELL IN LOVE WITH REFLEXOLOGY AND STARTED WORKING ON FAMILY AND FRIENDS AS OFTEN AS POSSIBLE. THE BEAUTY OF REFLEXOLOGY IS THAT YOU CAN USE THESE EASY-TO-LEARN TOUCH TECHNIQUES ON YOURSELF AND OTHERS.

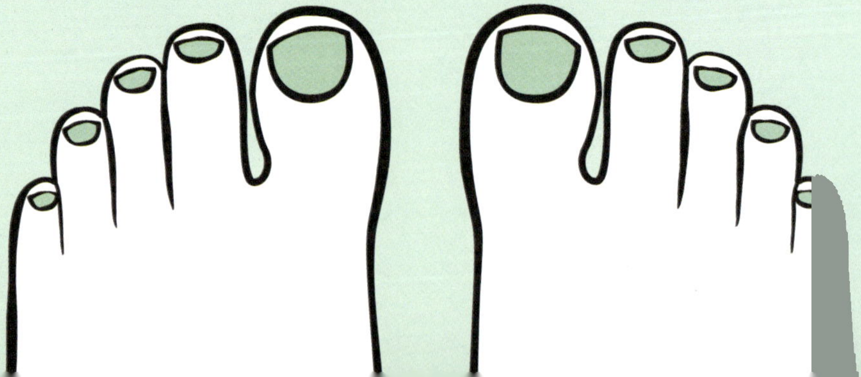

TODAY, AS A PROFESSIONAL CERTIFIED REFLEXOLOGIST AND REFLEXOLOGY TEACHER, IT IS STILL MY GREATEST JOY TO WORK WITH PEOPLE EVERY DAY AND SEE THEIR HEALTH IMPROVE IN SO MANY WAYS. IT IS A JOY AND HONOR TO SHARE MY PASSION FOR REFLEXOLOGY WITH THE BEGINNER AND HOME REFLEXOLOGIST AND WITH MY STUDENTS.

ENJOY THIS FUN AND EASY WAY TO EXPLORE THE ART OF FOOT REFLEXOLOGY.

STEFANIE SABOUNCHIAN

DISCLAIMER

ABOUT THIS BOOK

This practical illustrated guide to foot reflexology introduces a new and simple way of learning the art of reflexology for beginners and home reflexologists. The book explores one reflex point at a time – with color-coded illustrations showing where the reflex points are located on the feet, to which part of the body they correspond and how to apply the pressure techniques.

CHAPTER 1: *Basic Principles*

After exploring reflexology as a practice – how it works and its history – you will learn how the chain of benefits can assist in activating our body's self-healing ability, and when it is advised not to use reflexology. You will then be introduced to the 'map concept': the foot reflexology map as a micro-map of the human body.

CHAPTER 2: *Techniques*

In this hands-on section, you will learn the principles of using a variety of unique thumb and finger techniques, along with the most efficient and powerful reflexology-specific techniques.

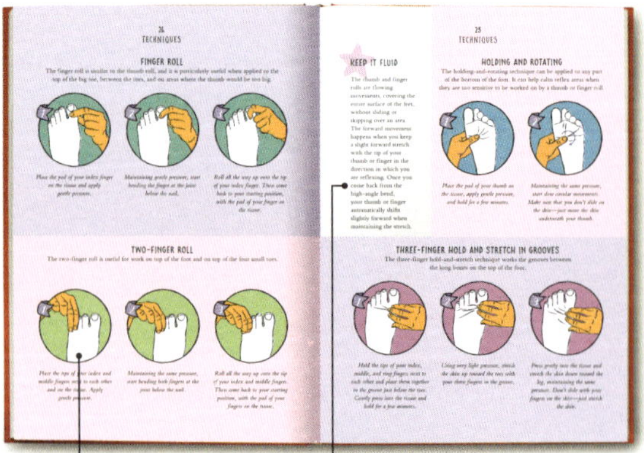

STEP-BY-STEP
TECHNIQUES ARE ORGANIZED INTO EASY-TO-FOLLOW STEPS.

HINTS AND TIPS
USEFUL TIPS ARE INCLUDED.

CHAPTER 3: *Reflex Points*

This main section invites you to explore each reflex point, from the top of the body to the bottom, color-coded by regions. Each double page is dedicated to one reflex point: illustrations on the right show where the reflex point is located on the foot; the left page gives instructions on how to apply the pressure techniques to that reflex point, the part of the body to which it responds and how reflexing the point can be beneficial.

TARGET
IDENTIFIES THE BODY PART THAT CORRELATES WITH THE FOOT REFLEX.

INSTRUCTIONS
DETAILED INSTRUCTIONS ON HOW TO WORK THE REFLEX AND WHICH TECHNIQUES TO USE.

BENEFITS
THE IMPORTANCE OF WORKING THIS REFLEX.

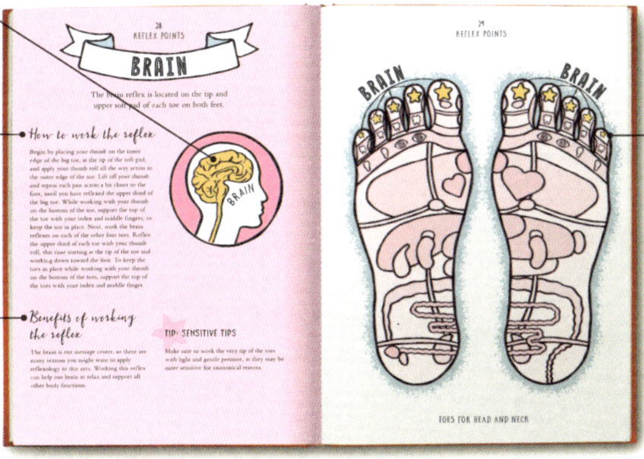

FOOT MAP
HIGHLIGHTS THE REFLEX LOCATION.

CHAPTER 4: *Ailment Directory*

An alphabetically organized ailment reference describes symptoms and the reflexes you can work for relief.

AILMENT LIST
EACH AILMENT IS FOLLOWED BY THE REFLEX POINTS YOU CAN WORK FOR RELIEF.

REFLEX POINTS
REFLEX POINTS ARE LISTED IN ORDER OF PRIORITY.

Contradindications and Precautions

Reflexology is considered safe when performed with gentle and nurturing touch and has no known side effects. Some conditions, however, may require you to adopt a precautionary practice or to avoid practice altogether.

Precautionary practice may involve using a lighter touch, or at least starting with a lighter touch to find out how the person responds.

There are situations when reflexology is considered a contraindication, and you should not use reflexology at all:

FIRST TRIMESTER PREGNANCY

✻ During this sensitive time, the fetus settles into the womb and you do not want to disturb that process in any way.

However, if the mother suffers from morning sickness, it is safe enough to very gently hold (but not work) the solar plexus point to ease the nausea.

AFTER ORGAN TRANSPLANT

✻ Reflexology should not be practiced for at least six months and until the new organ is accepted by the body. Even then, you should seek doctor's authorization before starting reflexology.

In some cases, it is advised to check with a healthcare provider before performing reflexology. You should seek medical authorization in the following cases:

TYPE 2 DIABETES

✻ Check with a healthcare provider before starting reflexology.

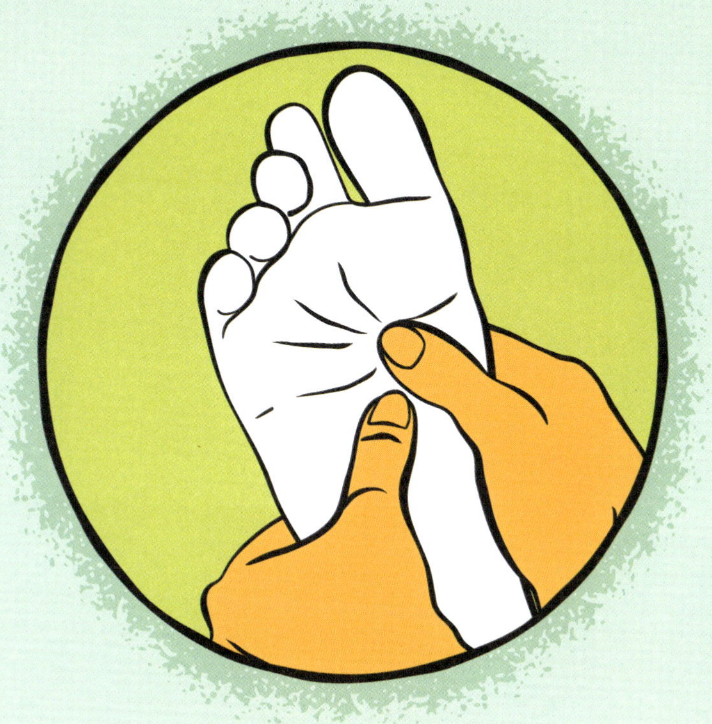

LYMPHATIC CANCER

✻ **Talk to the person's oncologist.**

Deep relaxation increases lymph flow, and cancer cells may be potentially carried through the body by the lymphatic vessels.

HAEMOPHILIA

✻ **Get doctor's authorization.**

If permission is granted, start with very light pressure, until you know how the person responds to reflexology.

ALTERNATING HIGH/LOW BLOOD PRESSURE

✻ **Get doctor's authorization.**

With deep relaxation, the person's blood pressure can change suddenly from very high to an extreme low.

DO NOT WORK DIRECTLY OVER:

- Varicose veins around the ankles
- Strains
- Sprains
- Broken bones
- Bone and joint injury
- Skin infections
- Broken skin
- Cuts
- Bruises and other skin conditions

1
BASIC PRINCIPLES

WHAT IS REFLEXOLOGY?

Through the simple touch of reflexology, we can help activate the body's self-healing ability in a safe and nurturing way.

Reflexology is a natural health approach to promote relaxation, increase circulation and balance the body's systems in a holistic manner.

The practice of reflexology is based on the concept of pressure maps, called reflexology maps, which resemble the shape of a human body and are found on the feet, hands and outer ears. Everything in the body, from top to bottom and front to back, has a corresponding reflex location on the feet, hands and ears.

The foot map is the most well-known reflexology map and is widely used around the world. Applying specific pressure techniques, using thumb and fingers on certain parts of the feet, can help a distant part in the body function more efficiently, as well as relieve pain and discomfort.

A bit of history

Although some form of footwork was known to ancient cultures, including China, India, Japan and Europe, written evidence of the reflexology map concept dates back to the early 1900s. Two American doctors documented an orderly arrangement of reflexes, closely resembling the shape of the human body, superimposed on the feet and hands. In 1917, William FitzGerald, MD, introduced a basic map concept of the Vertical Zone Theory. Joe Shelby Riley, MD, introduced the Horizontal Regions in 1924, after extensive study of Zone Therapy with Dr FitzGerald. Adding to FitzGerald's vertical zones, Riley's detailed documentation of the horizontal regions accelerated the development of modern reflexology. Over the years, a complex reflexology map, as we know it today, was developed.

Based on research

Since 1975, with the Danish Reflexology Association leading the way, research studies following scientific protocol have been conducted around the world, including China, USA, Spain, England, Denmark and Paraguay. In 1993, a reflexology research study, conducted by Bill Flocco of the American Academy of Reflexology, and Terry Oleson, PhD, Los Angeles, USA, was for the first time published in a scientific medical literature.

HOW REFLEXOLOGY WORKS

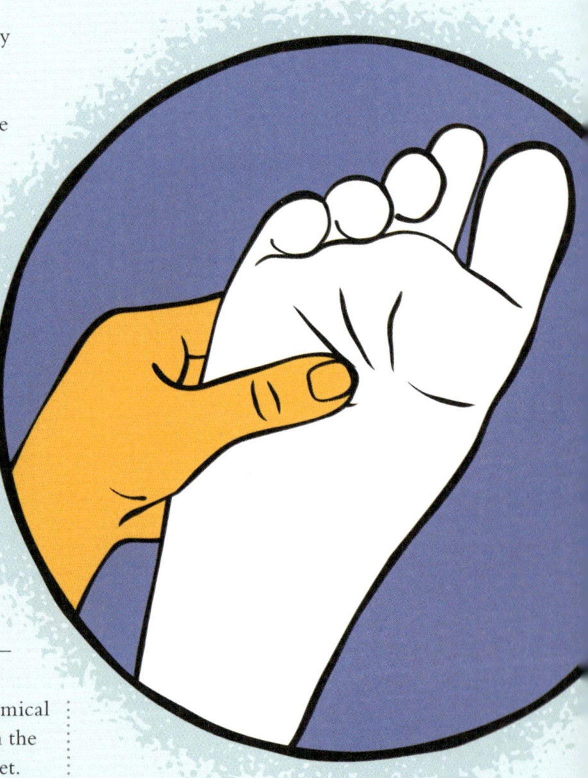

The main and most widely accepted theory on how reflexology works is through the nervous system. Research conducted by Jesus Manzanares, MD, Spain, supports the neurological theory. Biopsies taken from reflex areas on the feet, corresponding to body areas where people had health imbalances, showed increased nerve fibres in those reflex areas.

So what is the connection of your neck, shoulders, lungs and lower back to your feet? Messages travel through nerve pathways throughout the body, connecting the reflexology map on the feet with the corresponding parts of the body. There are more than 7,000 nerve endings in each foot. These nerves go up the legs, interconnecting with other nerves throughout the body. When health imbalances occur somewhere in the body – for example, tension in the lower back – blockages and congestions of different chemical types accumulate around nerve endings in the corresponding lower back reflex on the feet. It is suggested that one of these chemicals is 'Substance P', a neurotransmitter functioning as a pain transmitter. This accumulated deposit hinders the bio-electrical current from flowing freely through the nerve, partially blocking nerve messages.

By gently breaking down Substance P and other chemicals with specific techniques, the distant corresponding part of the body is also likely to experience some form of relief. Balance and health often returns to the affected area.

The power of touch

Another aspect we should not forget is the effectiveness of therapeutic touch. Soothing nerve endings on the feet with thumb and finger techniques not only breaks down blockages and congestions, but also helps increase circulation, deeply relaxing the whole body and improving body functions, thereby helping the person feel better overall.

THE BENEFITS

The list of reported benefits of reflexology is extensive. Many people around the world have experienced pain reduction, relaxation, better health through an improved immune system, vitality and so much more. Some of the many benefits of reflexology include:

Reduced stress

In our often hectic daily life, it can be difficult to stay relaxed and balanced. Prolonged stress takes its toll on the body and can cause illness. In a reflexology session, our body enters a deep state of relaxation, balancing mind and body and dissolving tension.

Improved circulation

When we are relaxed, our body's smallest blood vessels, the capillaries, open up and supply all of our cells with more oxygen and nutrients, which helps support cell function. This improves all body functions and enhances recovery after injuries and postoperative rehabilitation.

Optimized organ & gland function

Tension and stress cause organs and glands to become either overactive or underactive. With reduced stress, improved circulation and better cell function, our body is more likely to return to balance, helping organs and glands function more efficiently.

Strengthened immune system

Reflexology encourages the body to return to balance, promoting self-healing through relaxation and helping to normalize all of our functions, which, in turn, helps to improve our immune system. People who receive regular reflexology sessions report better health overall.

Relief from pain & discomfort

When we enter a state of deep relaxation in which stress and tension reduce, our body is able to produce certain chemicals to help ease or even eliminate pain.

Improved sleep

Many people report sleeping better after experiencing reflexology. When stress and tension leave the body, glands function at an optimal level, the mind is more balanced and the body is able to produce the important hormones needed for sleep.

Detoxification

Like any body work, reflexology helps the detoxification process. After blockages and congestions of different chemicals around nerve endings are broken down by using specific reflexology techniques, they are filtered by the kidneys and eliminated through urination.

The REFLEXOLOGY MAP

The reflexology map is a small map of the entire human body, in which every part in the body has a corresponding part on the feet. Or in other words, the part (feet) represents the whole (body). The right foot has all reflexes for the right side of the body and the left foot all reflexes for the left side of the body. Over the page are three more maps from different viewpoints. When working with the foot reflex map, keep in mind that every person is different – therefore, reflex locations may vary slightly from person to person. Use the map as a guideline and reflex broader areas to make sure that everything you want to work is included.

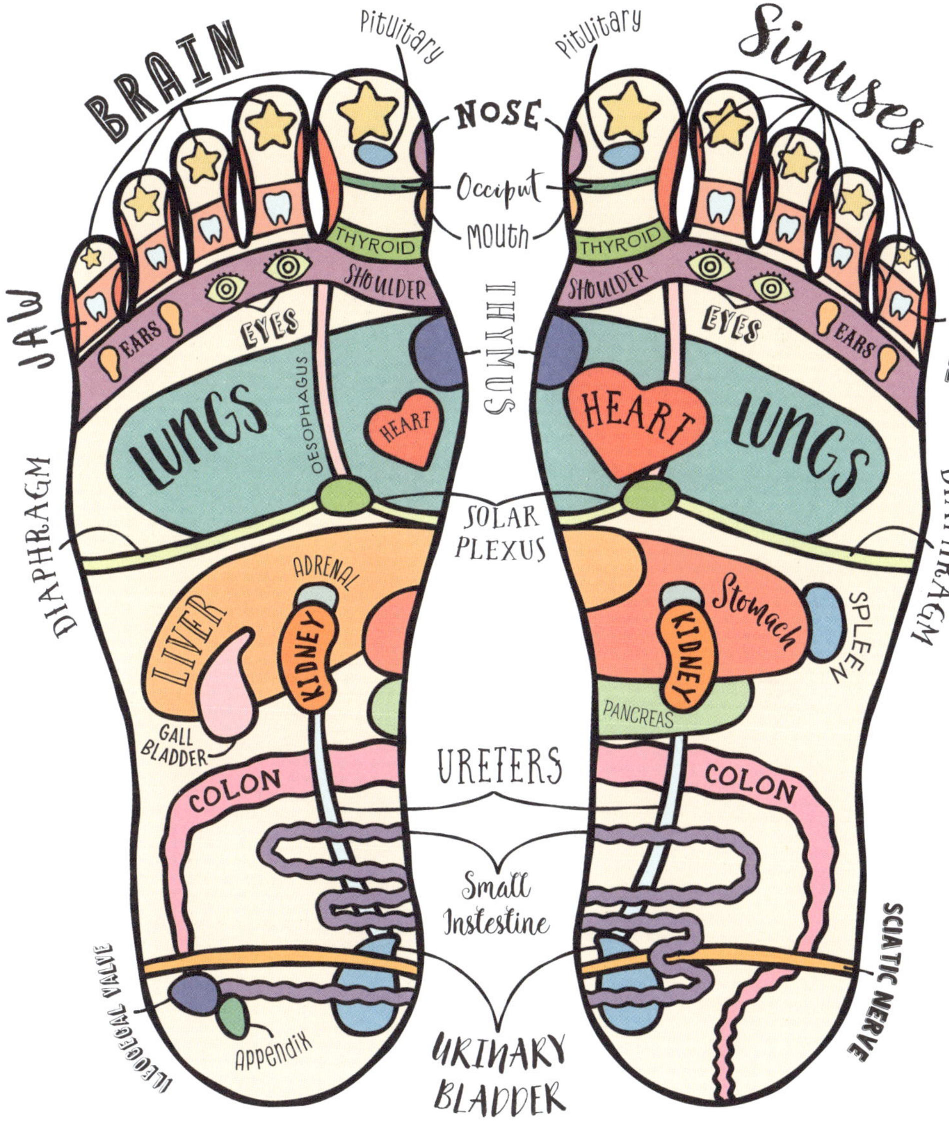

BOTTOM VIEW OF
RIGHT FOOT

BOTTOM VIEW OF
LEFT FOOT

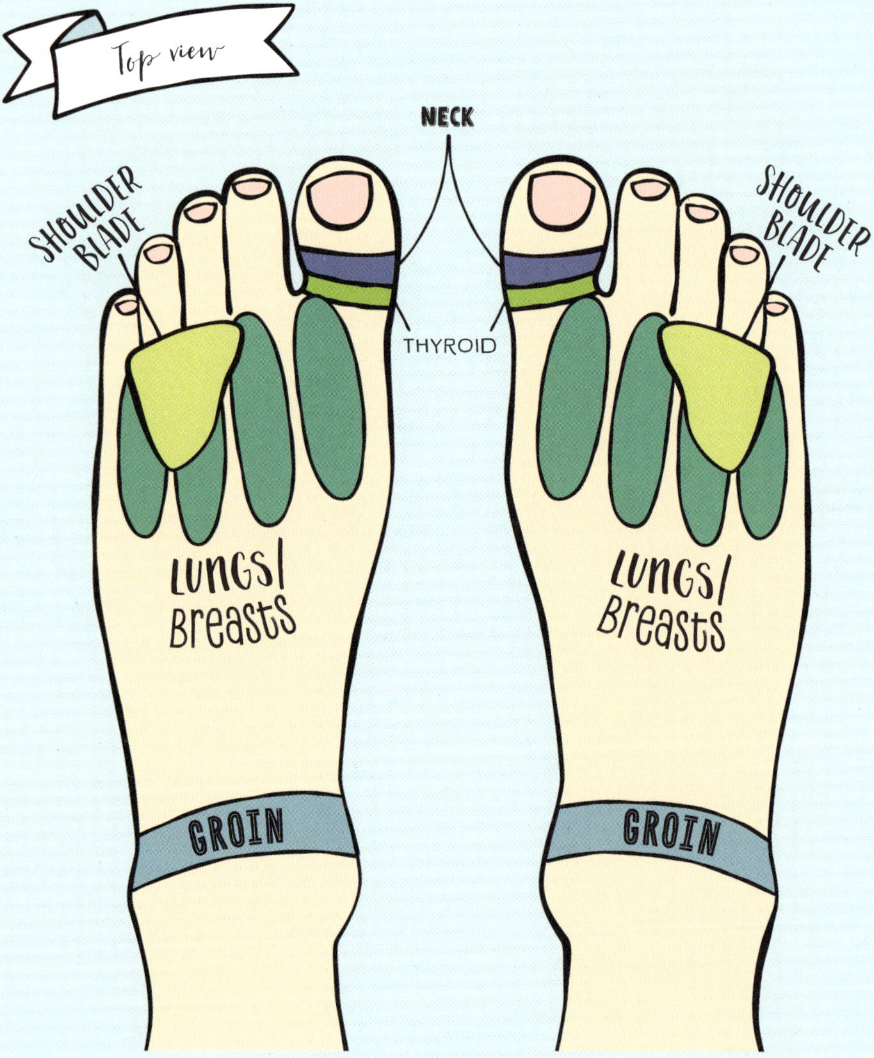
Top view
NECK
SHOULDER BLADE
SHOULDER BLADE
THYROID
LUNGS/ Breasts
LUNGS/ Breasts
GROIN
GROIN

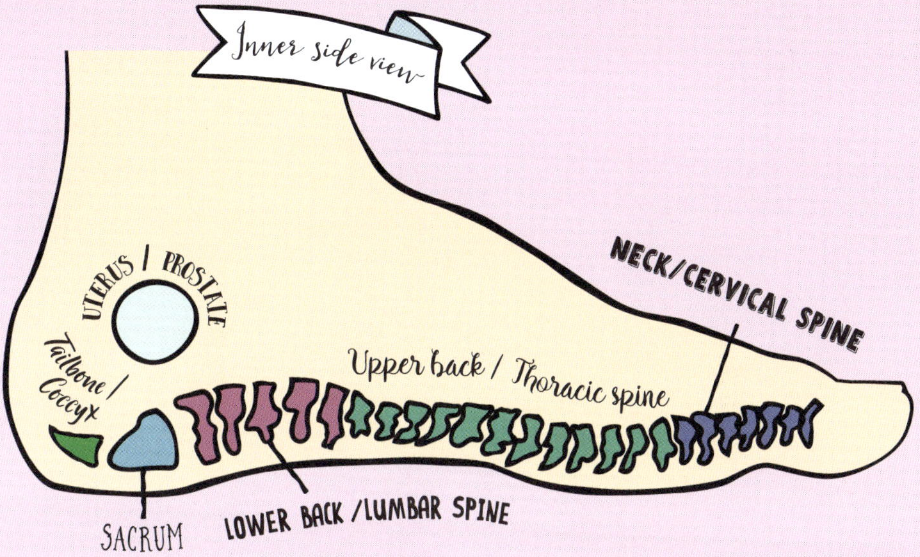
Inner side view
UTERUS / PROSTATE
NECK/CERVICAL SPINE
Upper back / Thoracic spine
Tailbone / Coccyx
SACRUM
LOWER BACK / LUMBAR SPINE

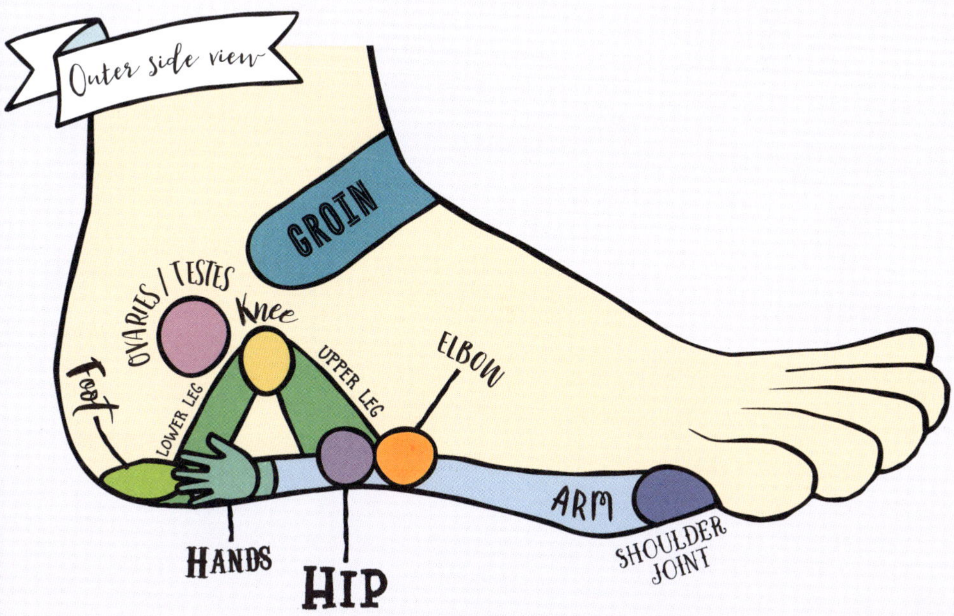
Outer side view
GROIN
OVARIES / TESTES
Knee
UPPER LEG
LOWER LEG
ELBOW
Foot
ARM
HANDS
HIP
SHOULDER JOINT

EXTRA REFLEX LOCATIONS

Shown on these two pages are the the two basic map concepts developed by Joe Shelby Riley and William FitzGerald; the Horizontal Regions and Vertical Zones are helpful guidelines for finding exact reflex locations on the feet.

How to use Horizontal Regions

Locate the region in the body where discomfort is experienced. Then look at your feet and find the corresponding region.

TOES for head and neck
BALL AND PAD for chest
SOFT SOLE for upper and mid abdomen
HEEL for lower abdomen and pelvic
INNER EDGE for midline and spinal
OUTER EDGE for arms and legs

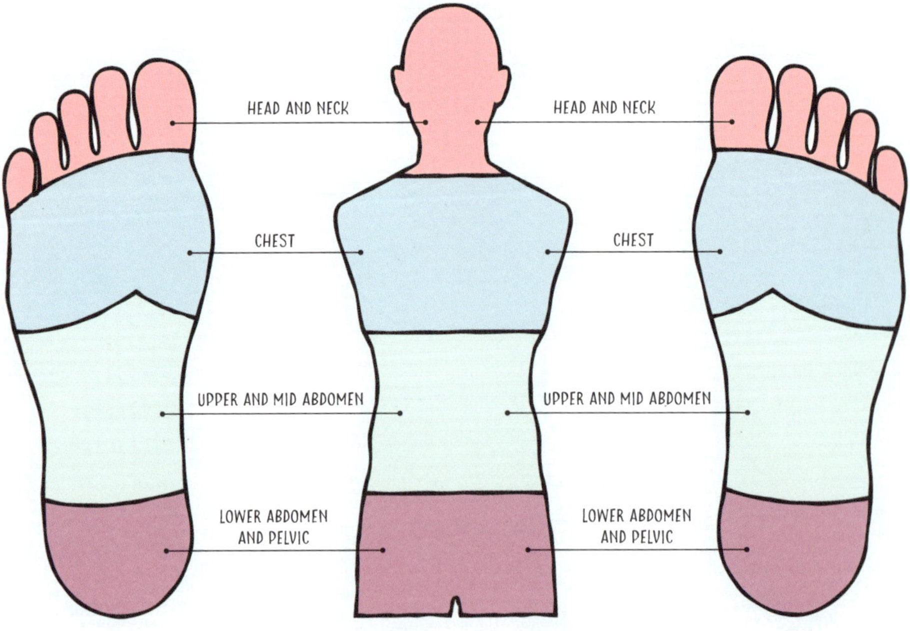

How to use Vertical Zones

Divide the body into 10 vertical zones, five on each side. Then look at the feet and also divide them into 10 vertical zones, five on each foot. Each zone in the body corresponds to the same zone on the feet.

After you have identified the region where discomfort is experienced, locate the zone in the body. Then look at your feet and find the corresponding zone.

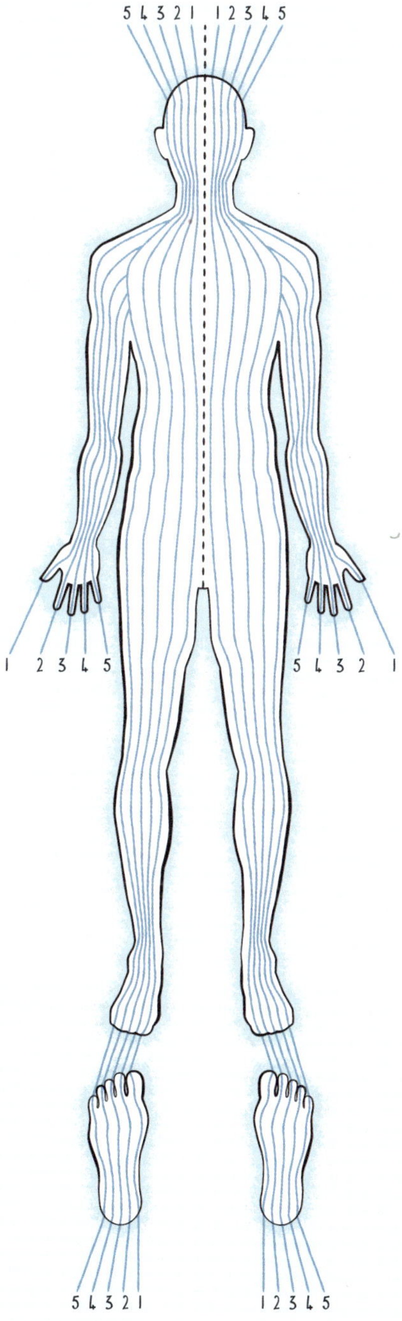

TIP: ACCESS ALL AREAS

These two simplified maps make it clear that you can work for everything in the body. In addition to organs, you can reflex for a sore muscle in the abdomen, for bruised ribs in the chest or for sunburn on the arm, to give just a few examples.

2

TECHNIQUES

REFLEXOLOGY TECHNIQUES

The practice of reflexology uses a variety of unique thumb and finger techniques. All of these techniques are small movements applied to the relatively small reflex map on the feet, and they are designed to soothe the nerves and to release blockages and congestions around nerve endings.

The thumb roll is the main technique you will be using. Other techniques are the finger roll, which can be done with one finger or two fingers next to each other, and a three-finger stretch, used in the grooves between the long bones on the top of the feet.

You can use all of these techniques on yourself and on someone else. Keep your fingernails short to avoid causing discomfort on the foot you are working on. The thumb roll direction, reflexing from inner to outer edge or from outer to inner edge, might change depending on whether you are working on yourself or on someone else. In addition, there might be times when it feels better for you to use a finger roll instead of a thumb roll when reflexing the toes. Always choose the most comfortable option for you.

THUMB ROLL

The thumb-roll technique works best on large areas on the bottom of the foot. With a slight modification, using mostly the tip of your thumb, you can also apply the thumb roll to the bottom of the toes.

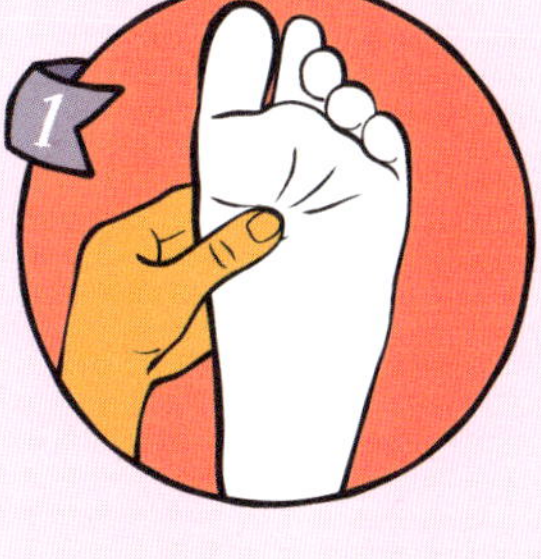

With a slight bend in the thumb, place the pad of your thumb on the tissue. Apply gentle pressure.

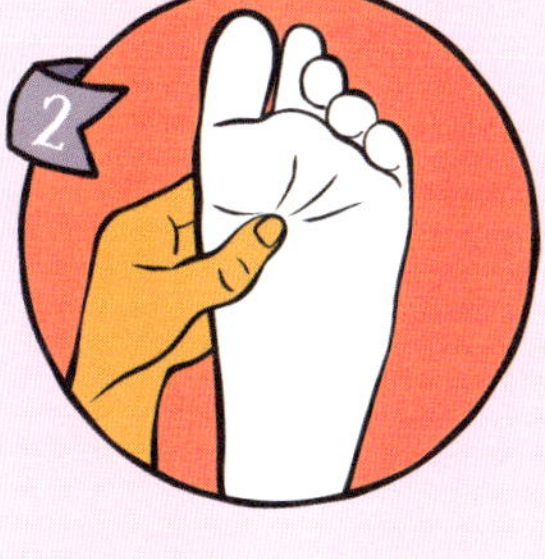

While maintaining the same pressure and keeping the tip of your thumb in the same place, start bending your thumb joint forwards.

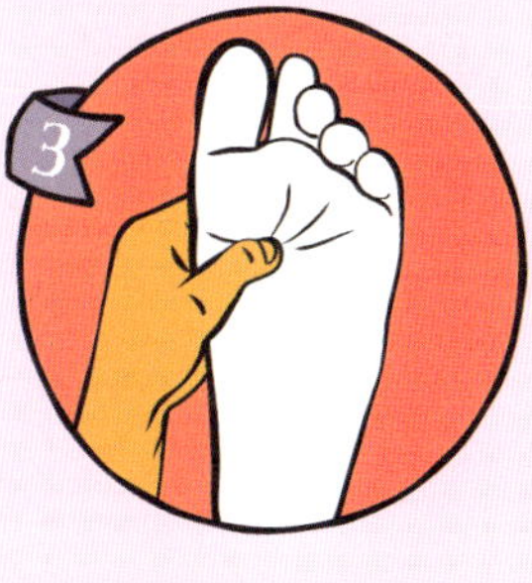

Roll up onto the tip of your thumb until it is bent to an almost 90° angle. Then come back to your starting position, with your thumb slightly bent.

FINGER ROLL

The finger roll is similar to the thumb roll, and it is particularly useful when applied to the top of the big toe, between the toes and on areas where the thumb would be too big.

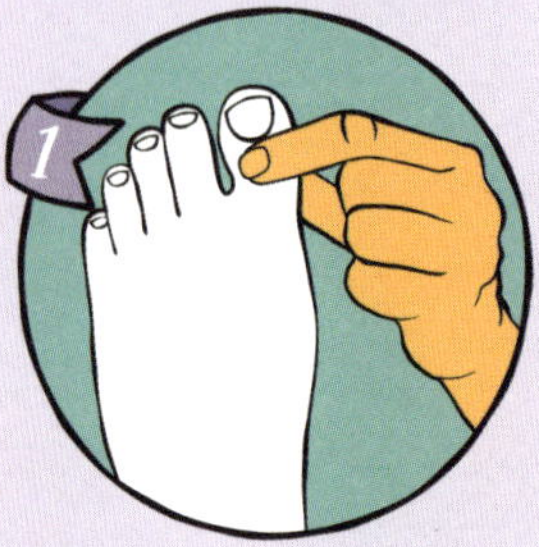

Place the pad of your index finger on the tissue and apply gentle pressure.

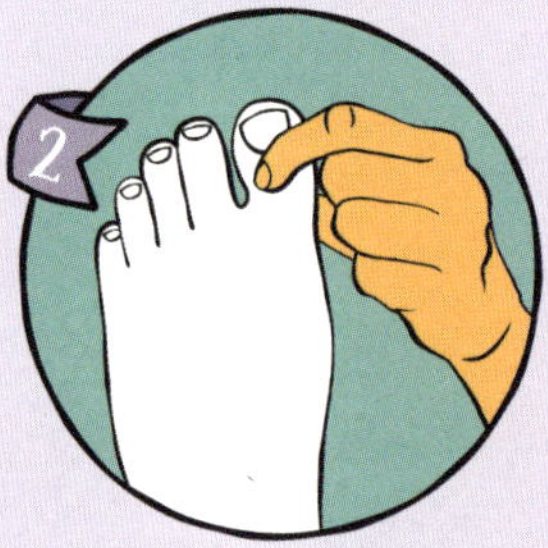

Maintaining gentle pressure, start bending the finger at the joint below the nail.

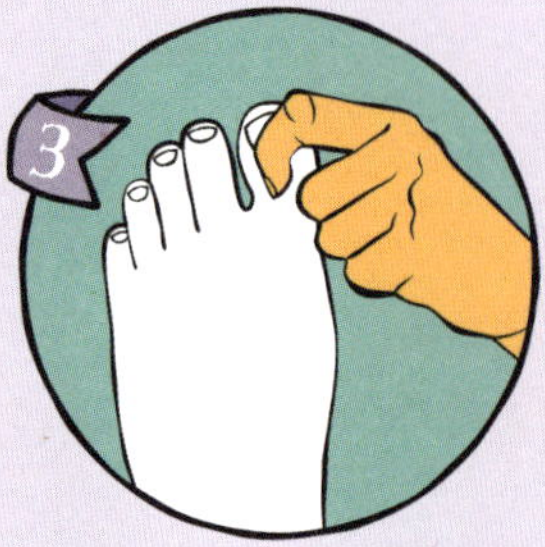

Roll all the way up onto the tip of your index finger. Then come back to your starting position, with the pad of your finger on the tissue.

TWO-FINGER ROLL

The two-finger roll is useful for work on top of the foot and on top of the four small toes.

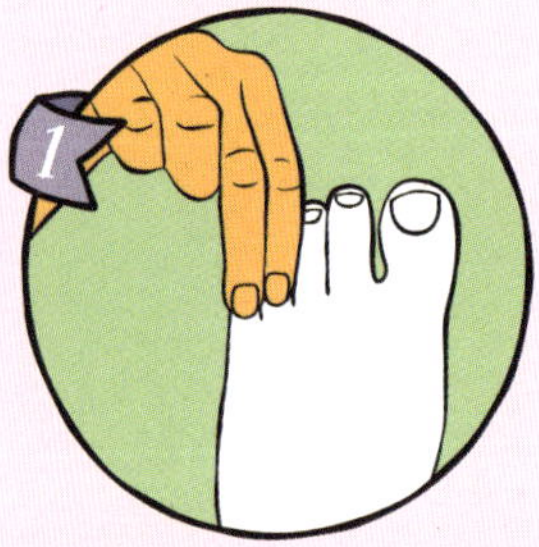

Place the tips of your index and middle fingers next to each other and on the tissue. Apply gentle pressure.

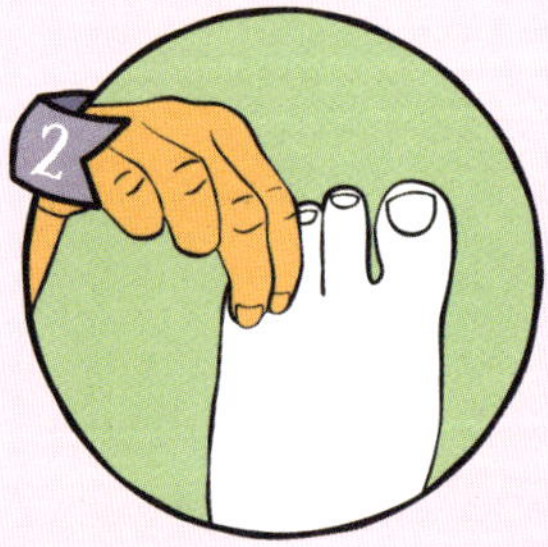

Maintaining the same pressure, start bending both fingers at the joint below the nail.

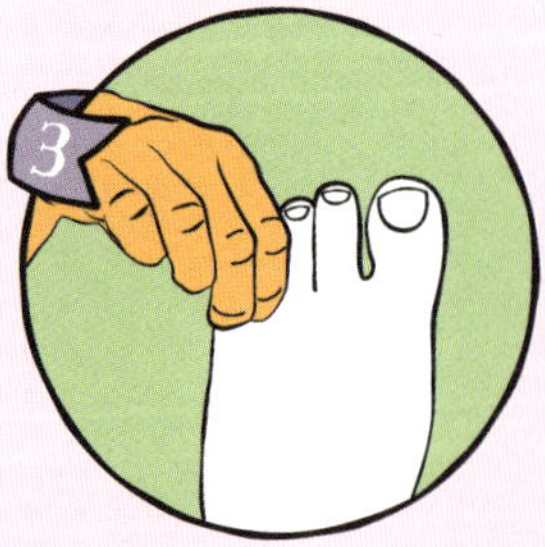

Roll all the way up onto the tip of your index and middle fingers. Then come back to your starting position, with the pad of your fingers on the tissue.

KEEP IT FLUID

The thumb and finger rolls are flowing movements, covering the entire surface of the feet, without sliding or skipping over an area. The forwards movement happens when you keep a slight forwards stretch with the tip of your thumb or finger in the direction in which you are reflexing. Once you come back from the high-angle bend, your thumb or finger automatically shifts slightly forwards when maintaining the stretch.

HOLDING AND ROTATING

The holding-and-rotating technique can be applied to any part of the bottom of the foot. It can help calm reflex areas when they are too sensitive to be worked on by a thumb or finger roll.

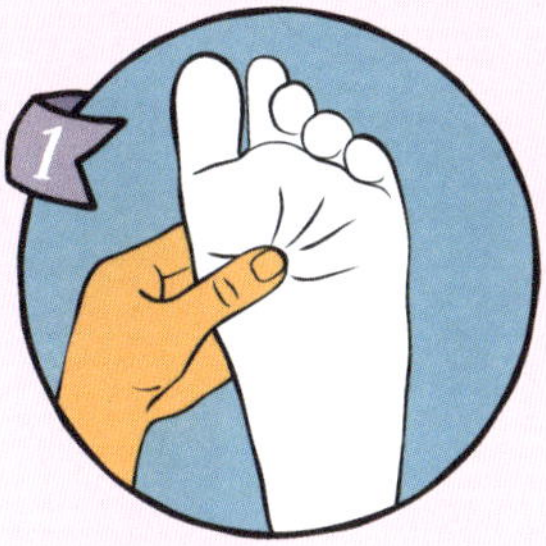

Place the pad of your thumb on the tissue, apply gentle pressure and hold for a few minutes.

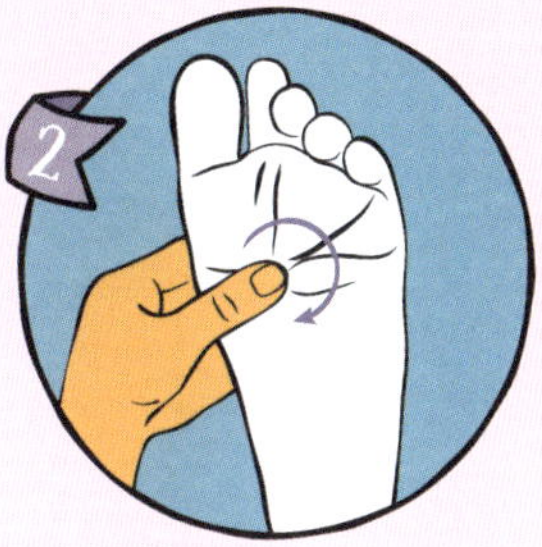

Maintaining the same pressure, start slow circular movements. Make sure that you don't slide on the skin – just move the skin underneath your thumb.

THREE-FINGER HOLD AND STRETCH IN GROOVES

The three-finger hold-and-stretch technique works the grooves between the long bones on the top of the foot.

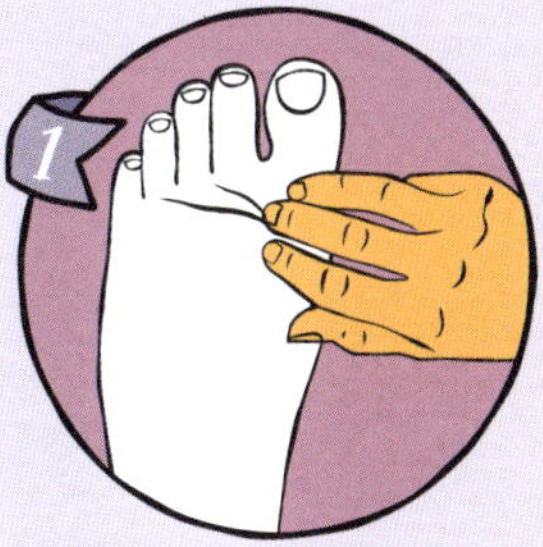

Hold the tips of your index, middle and ring fingers next to each other and place them together in the groove just below the toes. Gently press into the tissue and hold for a few minutes.

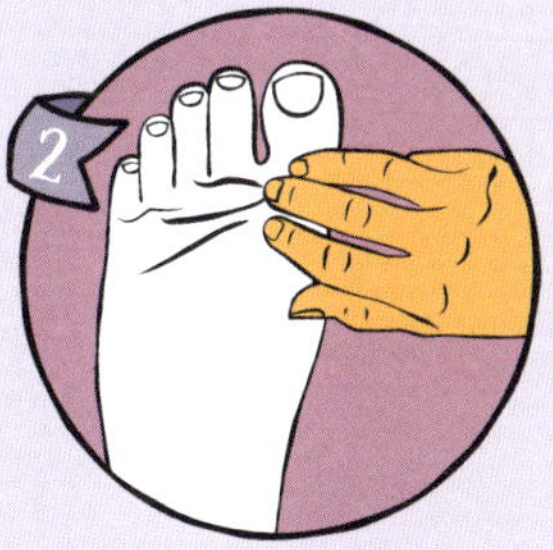

Using very light pressure, stretch the skin up towards the toes with your three fingers in the groove.

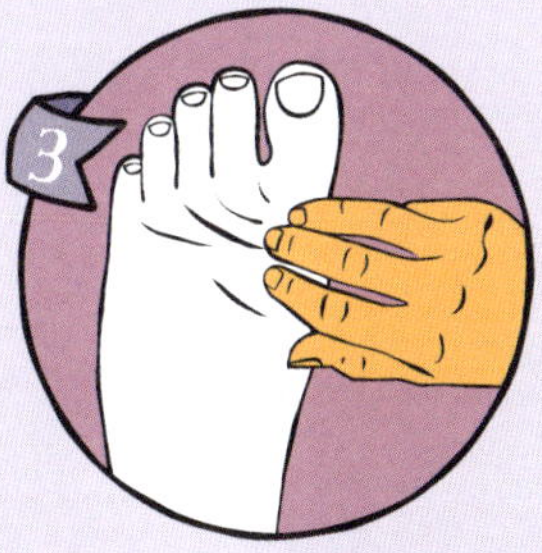

Press gently into the tissue and stretch the skin down towards the leg, maintaining the same pressure. Don't slide with your fingers on the skin – just stretch the skin.

3

REFLEX POINTS

BRAIN

The brain reflex is located on the tip and upper soft pad of each toe on both feet.

How to work the reflex

Begin by placing your thumb on the inner edge of the big toe, at the tip of the soft pad, and apply your thumb roll all the way across to the outer edge of the toe. Lift off your thumb and repeat each pass across a bit closer to the foot, until you have reflexed the upper third of the big toe. While working with your thumb on the bottom of the toe, support the top of the toe with your index and middle fingers, to keep the toe in place. Next, work the brain reflexes on each of the other four toes. Reflex the upper third of each toe with your thumb roll, this time starting at the tip of the toe and working down towards the foot. To keep the toes in place while working with your thumb on the bottom of the toes, support the top of the toes with your index and middle finger.

Benefits of working the reflex

The brain is our message centre, so there are many reasons you might want to apply reflexology to this area. Working this reflex can help our brain to relax and support all other body functions.

TIP: SENSITIVE TIPS

Make sure to work the very tip of the toes with light and gentle pressure, as they may be more sensitive for anatomical reasons.

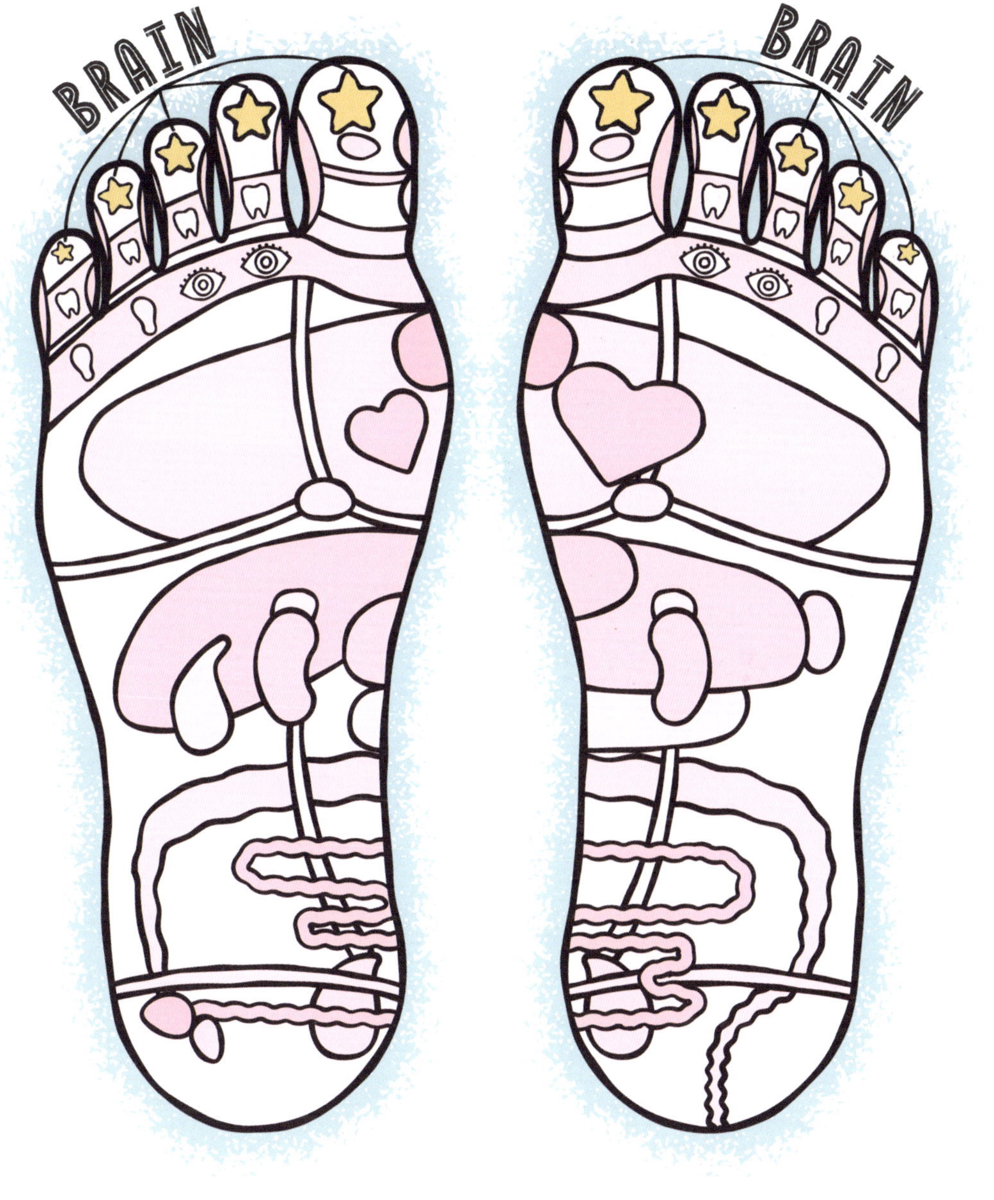

TOES FOR HEAD AND NECK

Pituitary

The pituitary reflex is located in the centre of the upper part of the big toe on both feet.

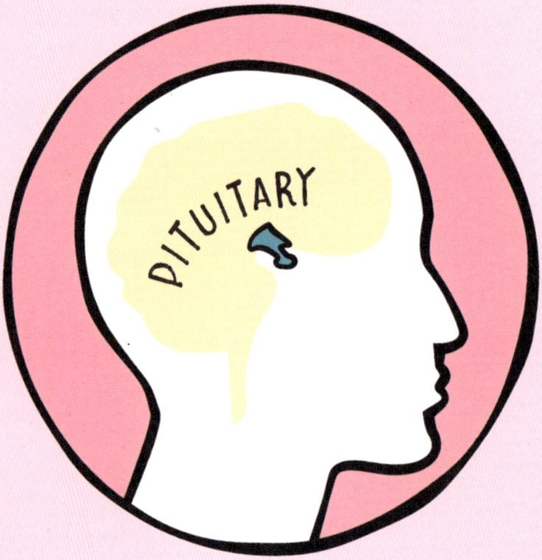

How to work the reflex

Place the pad of your thumb in the centre of the upper part of the left big toe. Hold the area for a couple of minutes, then start gentle circular movements with your thumb without leaving the pituitary reflex point. Alternate holding and circular movements for a few minutes. Then work the general area on and around the pituitary reflex with your thumb-roll technique. Repeat the same techniques on the right big toe.

TIP: VARY YOUR PRACTICE

Applying all three techniques – holding, circular movement and thumb roll – is optional, and doesn't have to be in this order.

Benefits of working the reflex

The pituitary plays an important role in regulating hormonal secretion in the body. Stimulating the pituitary reflex may help balance its function of secreting hormones, and help the entire endocrine system to work efficiently.

REFLEX POINTS

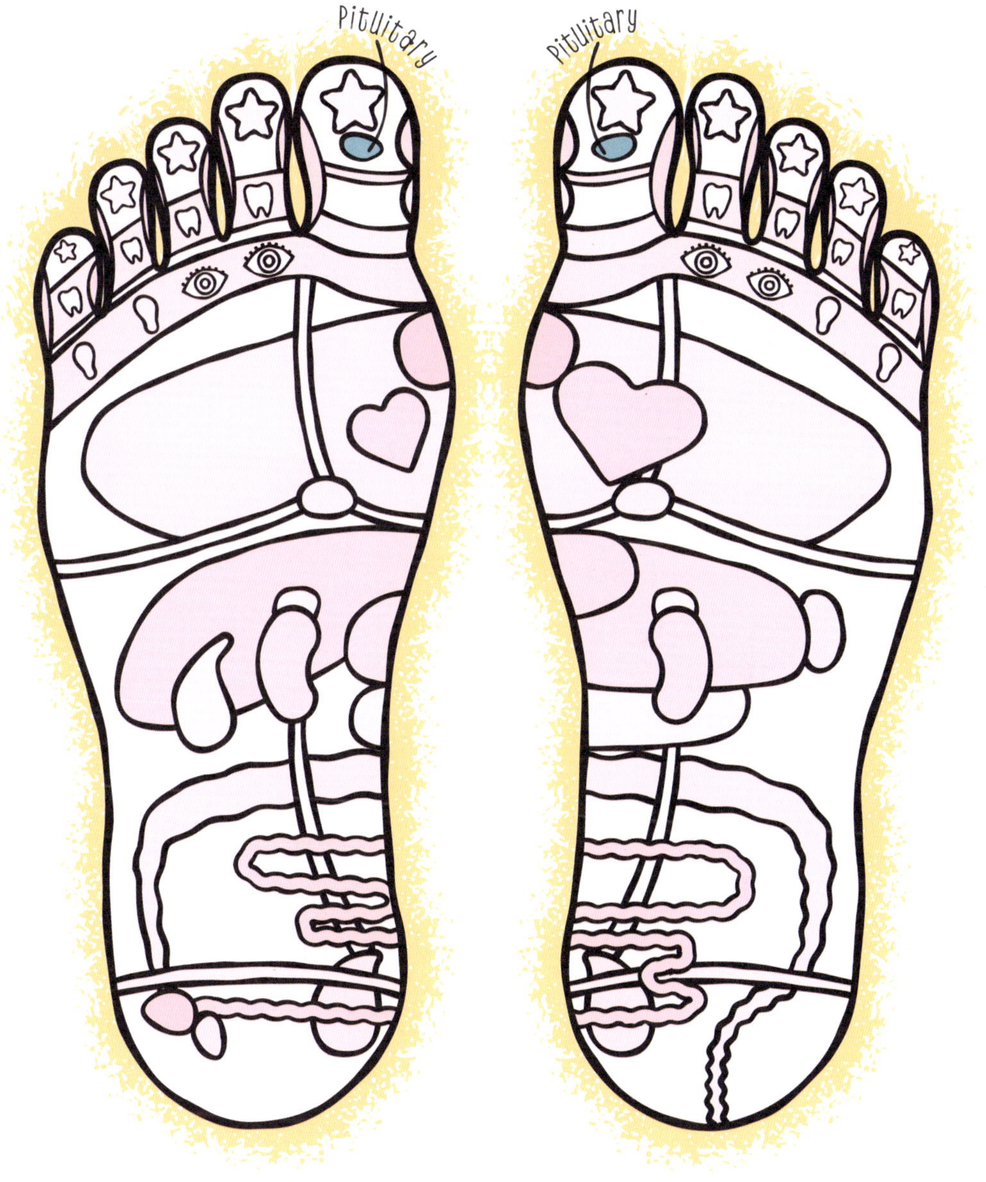

TOES FOR HEAD AND NECK

Occiput

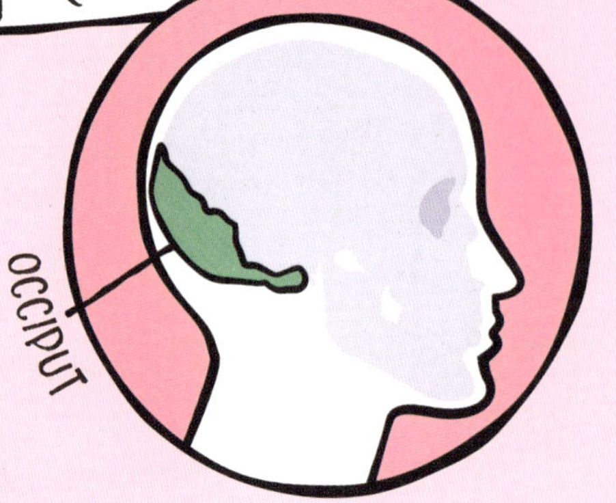

The occiput reflex is located on the joint of the big toe on both feet.

How to work the reflex

Always work both big toes when working the occiput reflex. Start by creating a platform with your index, middle and ring fingers side by side, to support the top of the left big toe. Next, place your thumb at the inner edge of the big toe, just above the joint. Apply your thumb roll horizontally across the bigtoe towards the second toe. With the following passes, work directly on and then below the joint.

After you have completed working the occiput reflex horizontally on and around the joint, continue by reflexing vertically. Again, begin by supporting the top of the big toe by cradling the upper half with your index, middle and ring fingers to keep the toe in place. Then place your thumb at the inner edge of the toe, just above the joint. Reflex with your thumb roll downwards over the joint. Continue until you have completed the area on and around the joint, all the way across the big toe. Repeat the same techniques on the right big toe.

Benefits of working the reflex

The occiput reflex on the joints of both big toes corresponds to the occiput, where the spine meets the head. Through reflexing the occiput, the muscles at this connection can be relaxed, which may help to relieve tension headaches – even migraines – and neck pain.

TIP: KEEP IT SMALL

Use small thumb-roll movements, and keep working the occiput reflex until the tissue on the joint becomes softer.

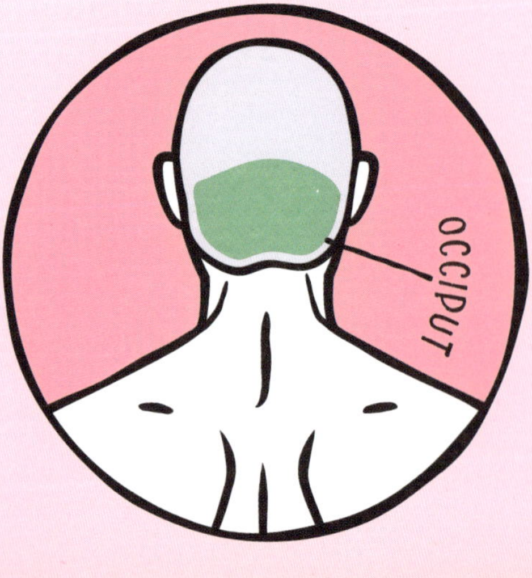

33
REFLEX POINTS

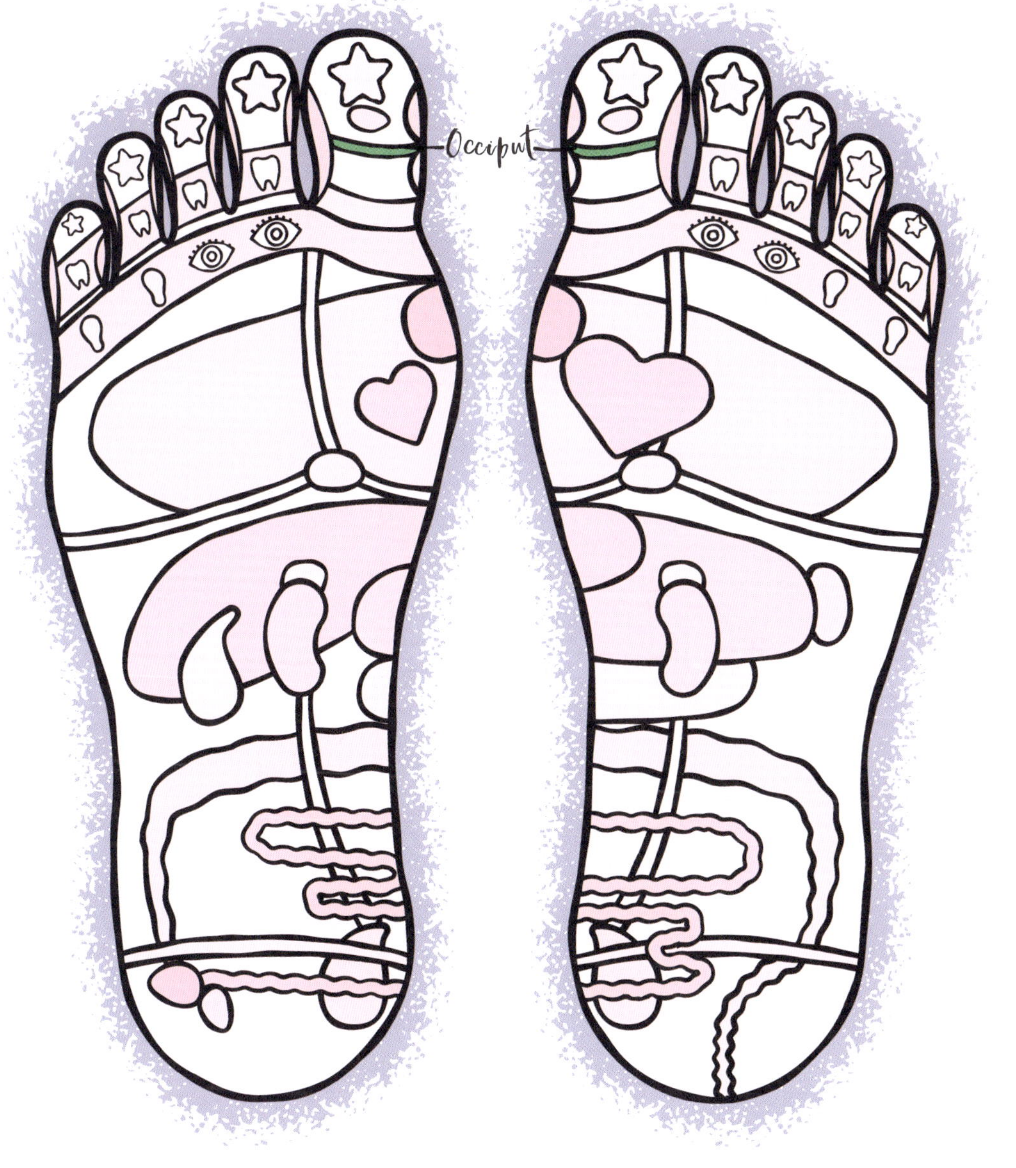

TOES FOR HEAD AND NECK

Sinuses

The sinus reflex is located on the sides and bottom of the toes on both feet.

How to work the reflex

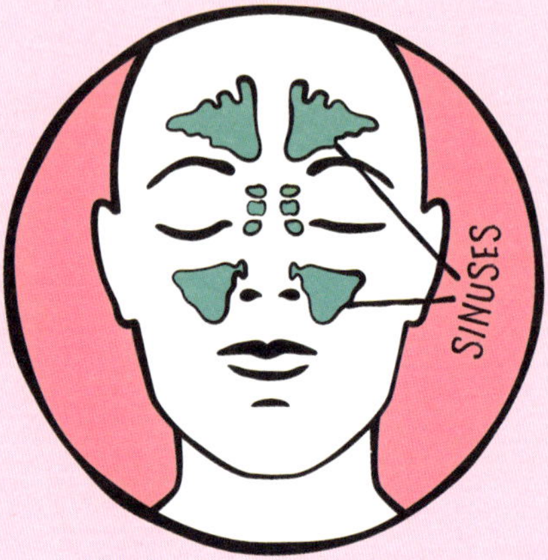

Begin with the left foot, working the inner side of each toe first. Start by creating a platform with your index, middle and ring fingers side by side, to support the top of the left big toe. Next, place your thumb on the inner edge of the big toe, near the tip, and work with your thumb roll down to the base of the toe. Continue working the inner side of all the remaining toes the same way.

After you have completed the inner side of each toe, work the outer sides, this time starting with the little toe. Again, start by creating a platform with your index, middle and ring fingers side by side, to support the top of the left little toe. Next, place your thumb on the outer edge of the little toe, near the tip, and work with your thumb roll down to the base of the toe. Continue working the outer side of all the remaining toes with the same technique.

After completing both sides, work the bottom of the toes. Begin by supporting the top of the big toe with your index, middle and ring fingers side by side. Place your thumb near the tip of the toe, close to the inner edge, and work with your thumb roll down to the base of the toe. Lift off and start again, this time a little closer to the outer edge, and continue working until you have covered the entire bottom of the big toe. Reflex the bottom of the remaining toes in the same way.

Repeat the above techniques on all of the toes of the right foot.

Benefits of working the reflex

There are four pairs of sinuses, a connected system of hollow cavities in the skull with a thin layer of mucus. Working the sinus reflex can bring relief from congestion, sinus-induced headaches, sinus infections and allergies.

TIP: KEEP IT SMALL

Use small thumb-roll movements when reflexing the sides and bottoms of the toes.

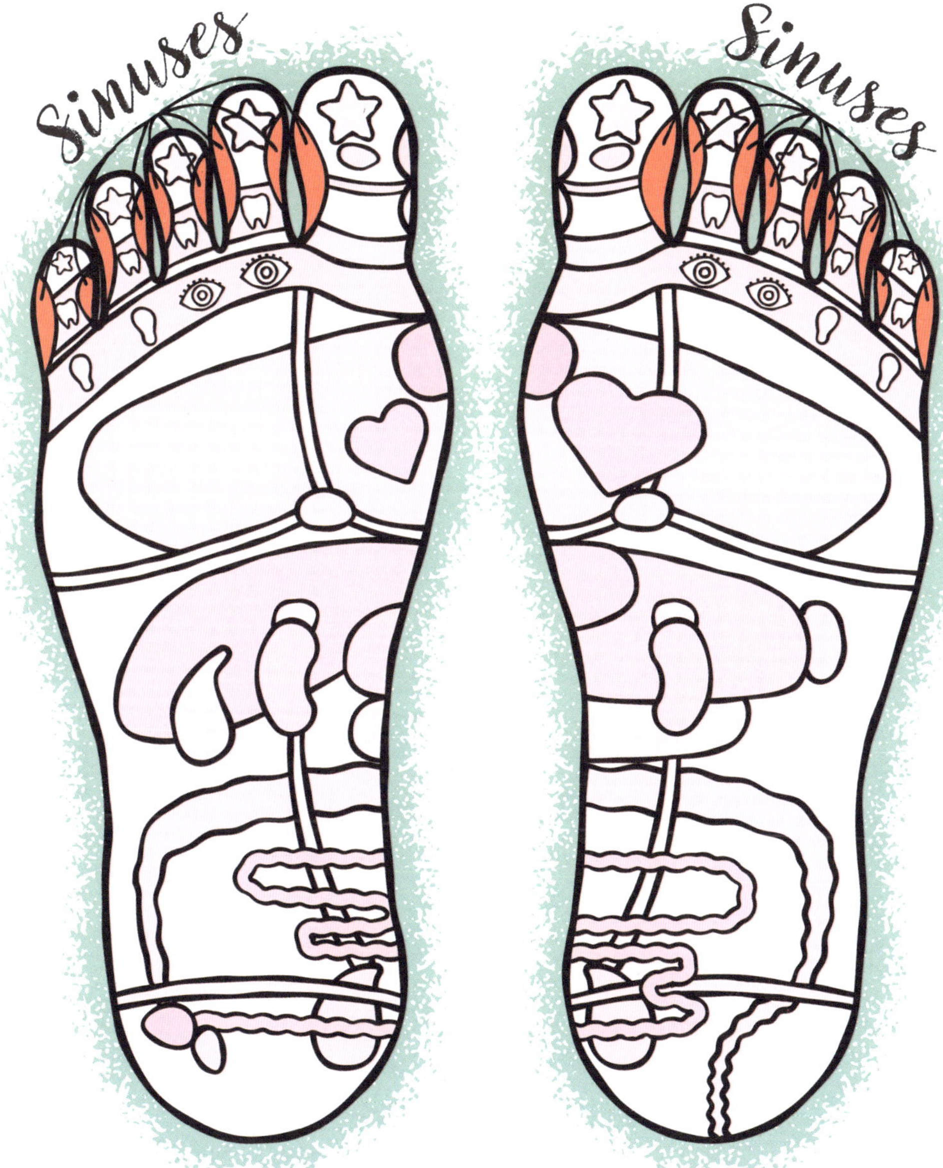

TOES FOR HEAD AND NECK

TEETH

The teeth reflex is located on the bottom of the four smaller toes on both feet, on the first joint close to the foot. The reflex is also on top of the big toes, between cuticle and joint, close to the nail.

How to work the reflex

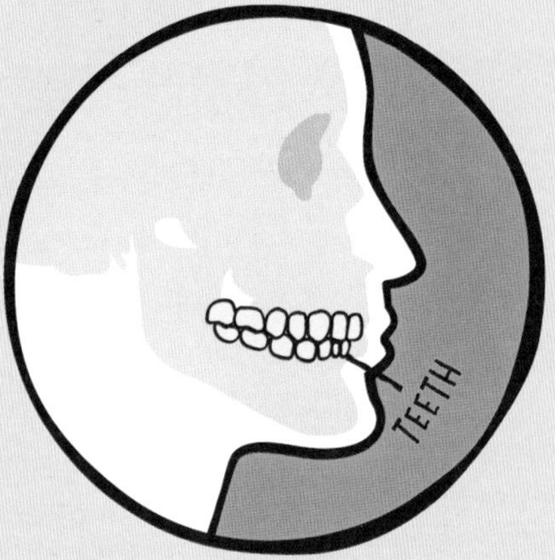

Begin by working the teeth reflex of the corresponding foot to the side of the mouth in which pain is being experienced. Reflex the joints of the four smaller toes first. Place the pad of your thumb on the bottom of the second toe, on the first joint. Work with your thumb roll across the toe and repeat several times. Next, apply the same technique on the third, fourth and fifth toes. After you have completed the bottom of the four smaller toes, reflex the top of the big toe. Place the pad of your thumb at the inner edge of the big toe, just below the cuticle, close to the nail. Work with your thumb roll all the way across the big toe. Lift off your thumb and start the next pass across a little closer to the foot. Continue until you have reached the joint. Repeat the same technique in the same areas of all the toes on the other foot.

Benefits of working the reflex

Working the teeth reflex can help relieve toothache. Be aware that toothache indicates an underlying issue that should be addressed by a dentist as soon as possible.

TIP: USE LIGHT PRESSURE

Be aware that the joints at the bottom of the toes can be very sensitive. Start with light pressure and hold any sensitive area until tenderness eases. Use the tip of your thumb when applying the thumb roll to the bottom of the four smaller toes.

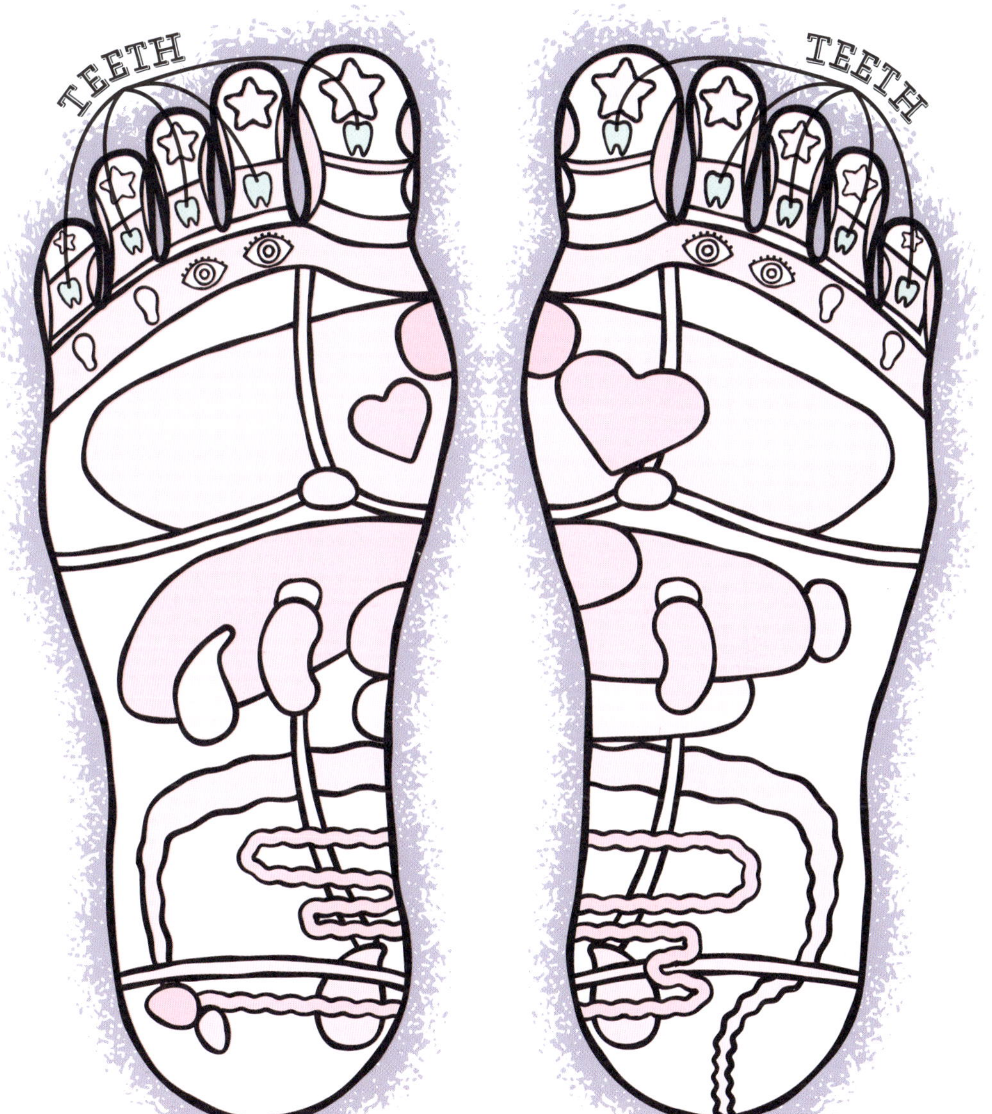

TOES FOR HEAD AND NECK

JAW

The jaw reflex is located on the top and bottom of all toes, on and around the first joint close to the foot.

How to work the reflex

If experiencing jaw or temporomandibular joint (TMJ) discomfort on one side, begin by working the jaw reflex of the corresponding foot, reflexing the joint of the big toe first. Place the pad of your thumb at the inner edge of the big toe, just above the joint. Work with your thumb roll towards the other toes, all the way across the big toe. Lift off your thumb and start again at the inner edge, this time directly on the joint. On the next pass across, reflex below the joint. Apply the same technique on the remaining four toes, on and around the first joint. After you have completed the bottom of the toes, work the top of all toes, on and around the first joint, using the same technique.

For additional work on the TMJ, repeat the work on the bottom of the big toe, on and around the joint, several times. Use the same thumb-roll technique, with special emphasis on the outer half of the big toe.

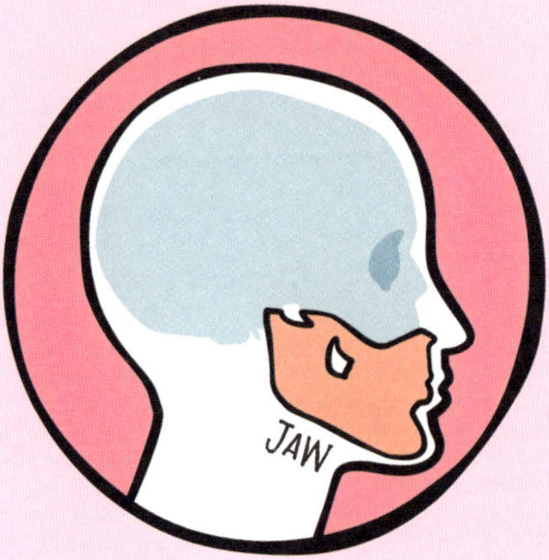

Benefits of working the reflex

Muscles help the lower jaw, also called the mandible, to move in all directions. The TMJ connects the skull to the lower jaw under the ear. Working the jaw reflex can help relax the jaw muscles and relieve pain and discomfort.

TIP: START LIGHTLY

The joints on the bottom of the toes can be sensitive, so begin with light pressure and hold any sensitive area until any tenderness eases. When applying the thumb roll on the bottom of the four smaller toes, use mostly the tip of your thumb.

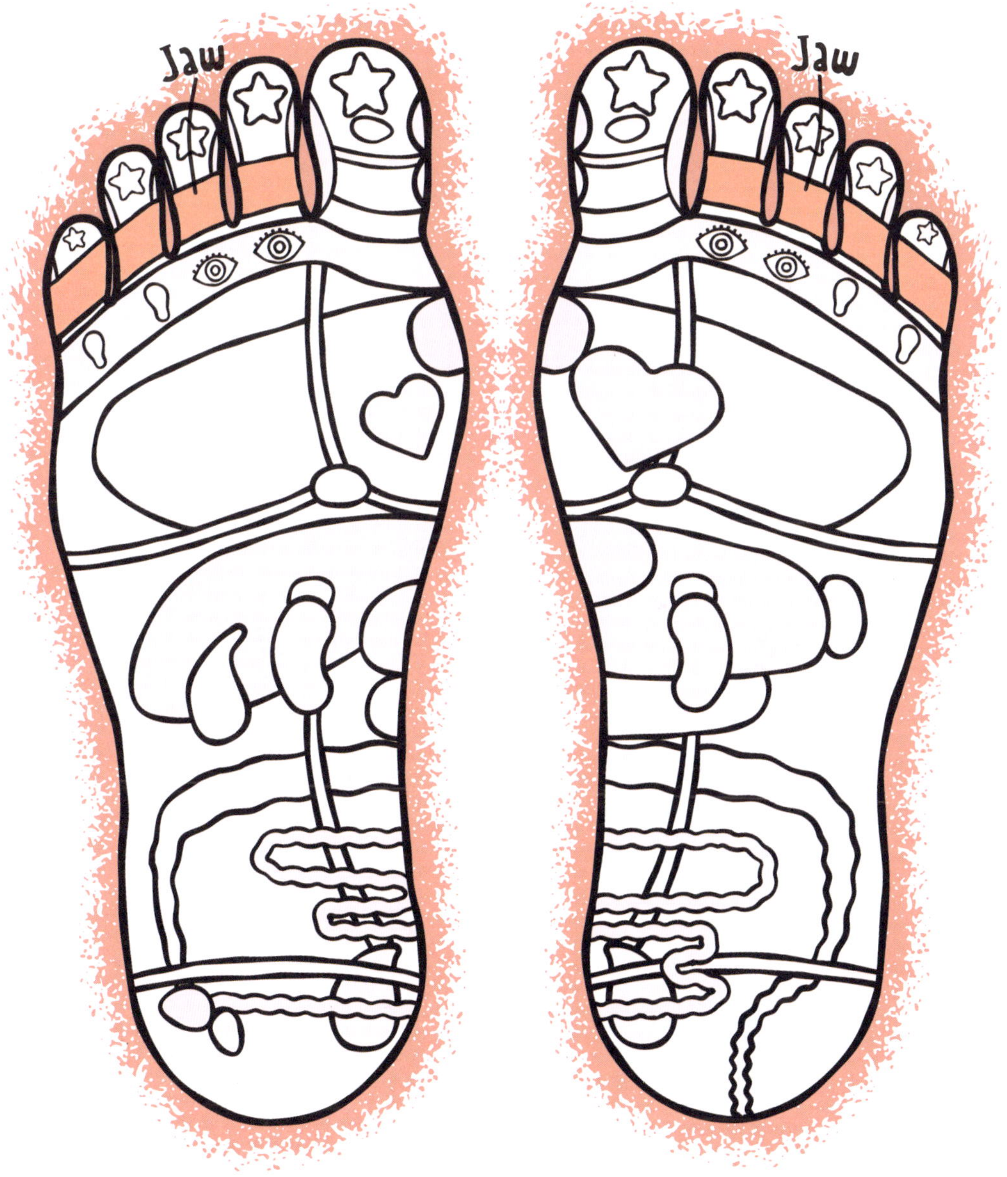

TOES FOR HEAD AND NECK

THYROID

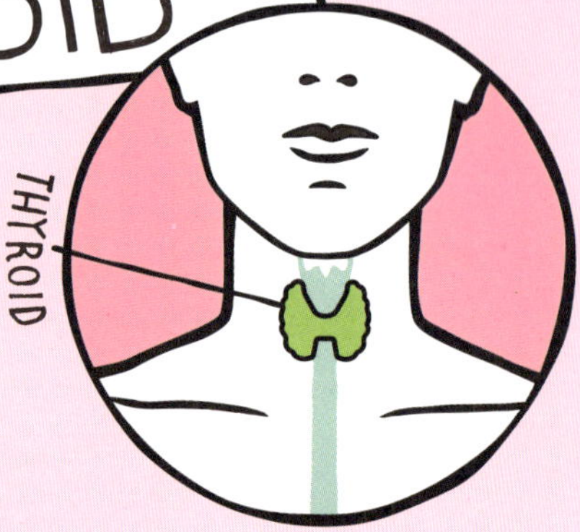

The thyroid reflex is located on the lower half of both big toes, on the top and bottom of the feet.

How to work the reflex

With your index, middle and ring fingers, create a platform on top of the left big toe to keep it in place while reflexing the bottom of the toe. Start your thumb roll at the inner edge of the big toe, below the joint, working across the entire toe towards the second toe. Lift off your thumb and start the next pass across a little closer to the foot. Continue reflexing horizontally until you have completed all of the lower part of the big toe. Next, use your index finger to work the thyroid reflex on top of the big toe. Place your thumb on the bottom of the toe to keep it in place. Start your finger roll at the inner edge of the big toe, below the joint, working across the entire toe towards the second toe. After completing both the top and bottom of the left big toe, reflex the lower half, top and bottom, of the right big toe with the same thumb and finger rolls.

Benefits of working the reflex

The thyroid, a large gland in the neck, plays a vital role in producing hormones that regulate the body's metabolism, blood calcium levels, and more. Working the thyroid reflex may help improve its many functions.

TIP: EXPLORE CAREFULLY

Be aware that the top of the big toe has less padding and you may feel tendons and blood vessels beneath the skin while reflexing. Begin your index finger roll with light pressure to explore the top of each toe you are working on.

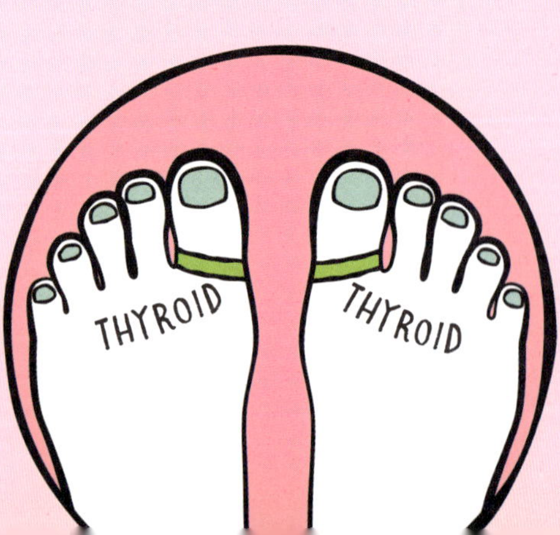

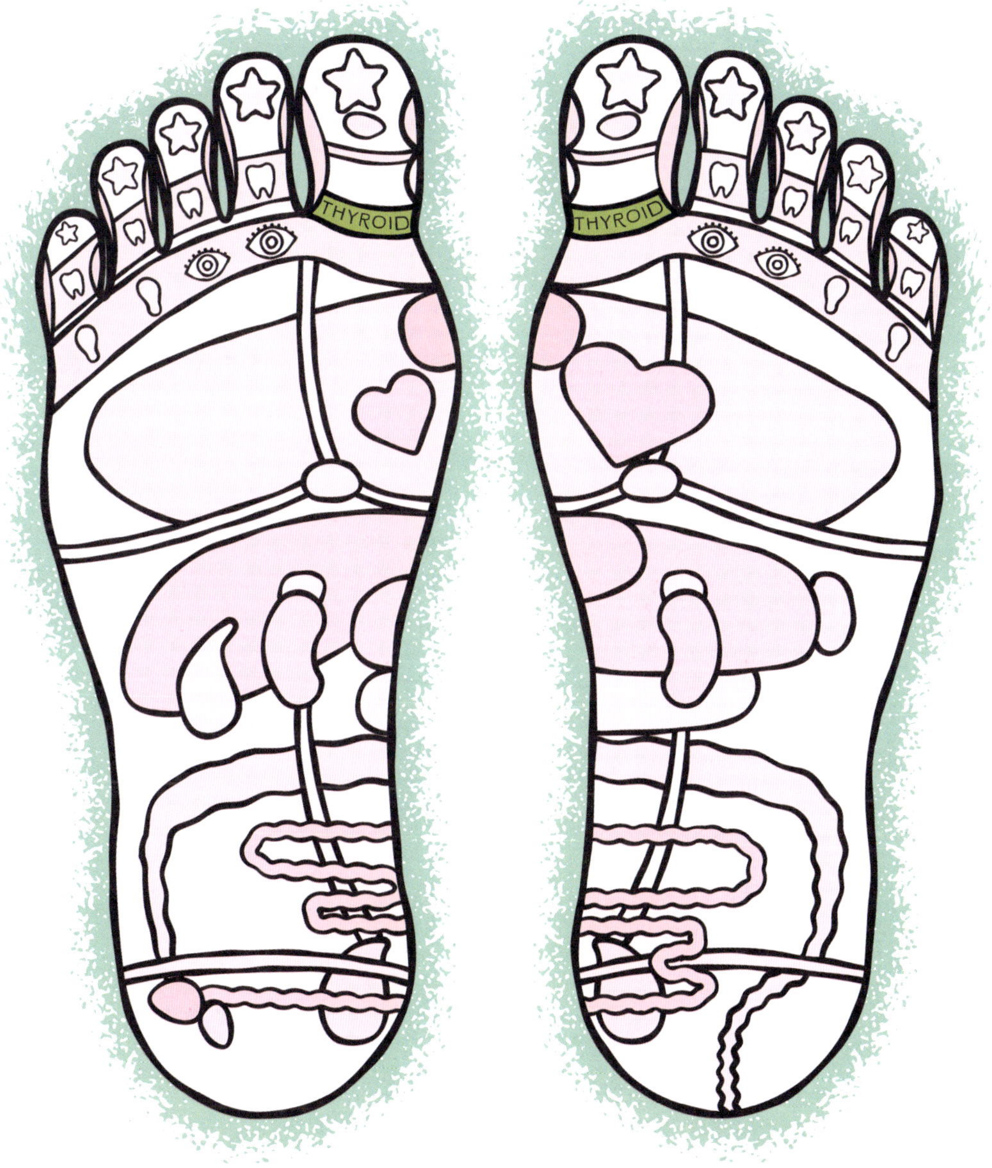

TOES FOR HEAD AND NECK

EYES

The eye reflex is located directly underneath the second and third toes of both feet.

How to work the reflex

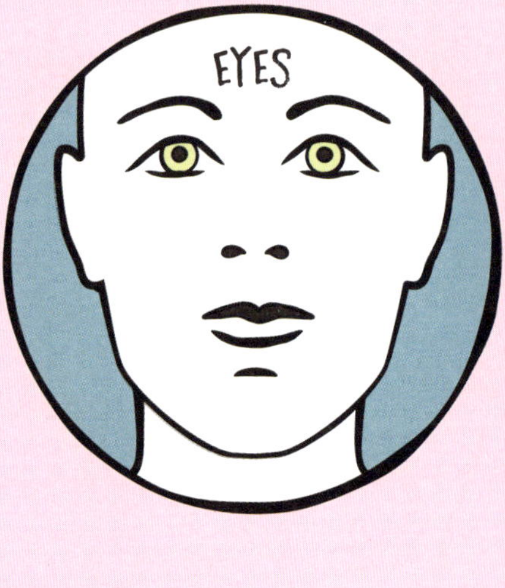

Beginning with the left foot, place the pad of your thumb directly underneath and between the third and fourth toes. Start thumb-rolling towards the inner edge, staying close to the toes, until you have covered the area below the third and second toes. After working in this direction a couple of times, reverse the direction. For extra emphasis, work upwards by starting your thumb roll slightly below the toe, continuing until you have reached the base of the toe. Apply the same techniques to the eye reflex of the right foot.

Benefits of working the reflex

Our eyes are easily strained – long hours at the computer, driving, or not getting enough sleep are common causes. Working the eye reflex can help ease tiredness of the eyes.

TIP: STAY ON THE TIP

Working the eye reflexes is most effective when using only the tip of your thumb, rolling with small movements over the tissue.

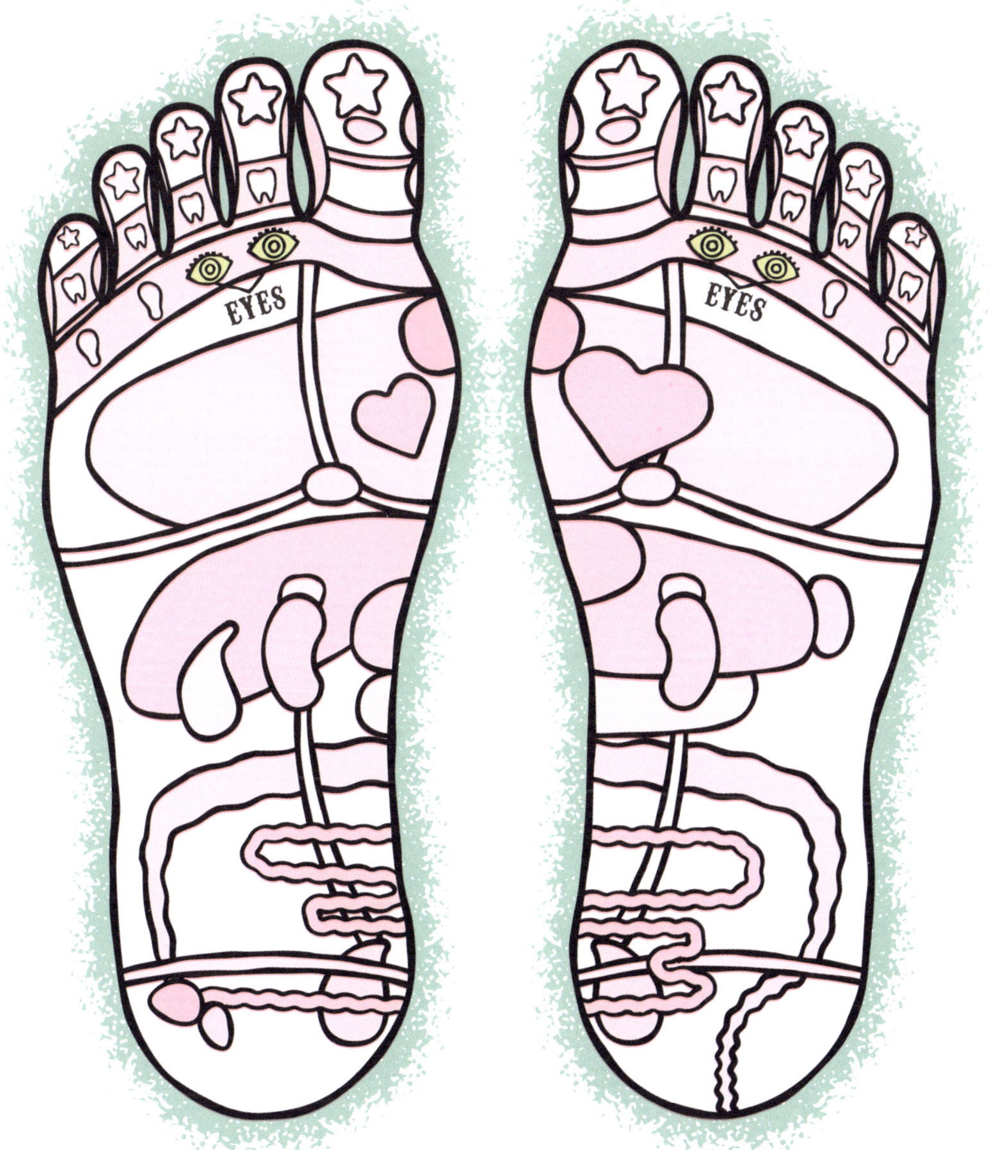

TOES FOR HEAD AND NECK

EARS

The ear reflex is located directly below the fourth and the fifth toe of both feet.

How to work the reflex

Begin by placing the pad of your thumb at the outer edge of the left foot, directly below the fifth toe. Thumb-roll towards the inner edge, until you have covered the area below the fifth and fourth toes. Make sure that you stay close to the toes, working directly below them. After reflexing a few passes, reverse the direction and work the same area, now from the fourth to the fifth toe. For extra emphasis, thumb-roll upwards by starting slightly below the toe, until you have reached the base of the toe. Do this technique for both the fourth and fifth toes, and then apply all of the techniques to the ear reflex of the right foot.

If you want to address issues in the inner ear, emphasize the work below the fourth toe and include the third toe, applying the same techniques described above.

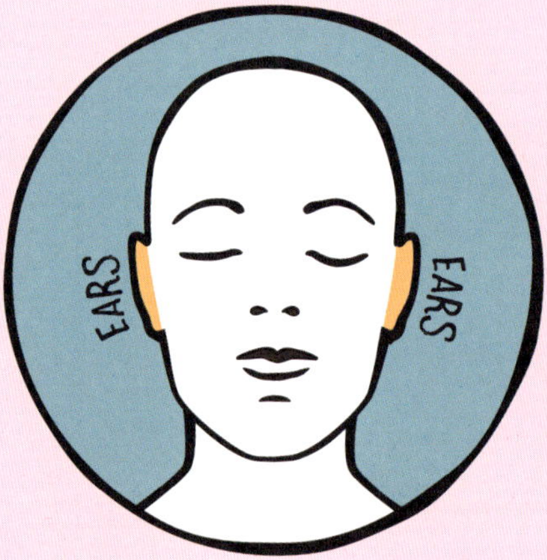

Benefits of working the reflex

Working the ear reflex can help to ease ringing in the ears (tinnitus) and may assist in the healing of ear infections.

TIP: KEEP IT SMALL

For best results, use the tip of your thumb and roll with small movements over the area of the ear reflex.

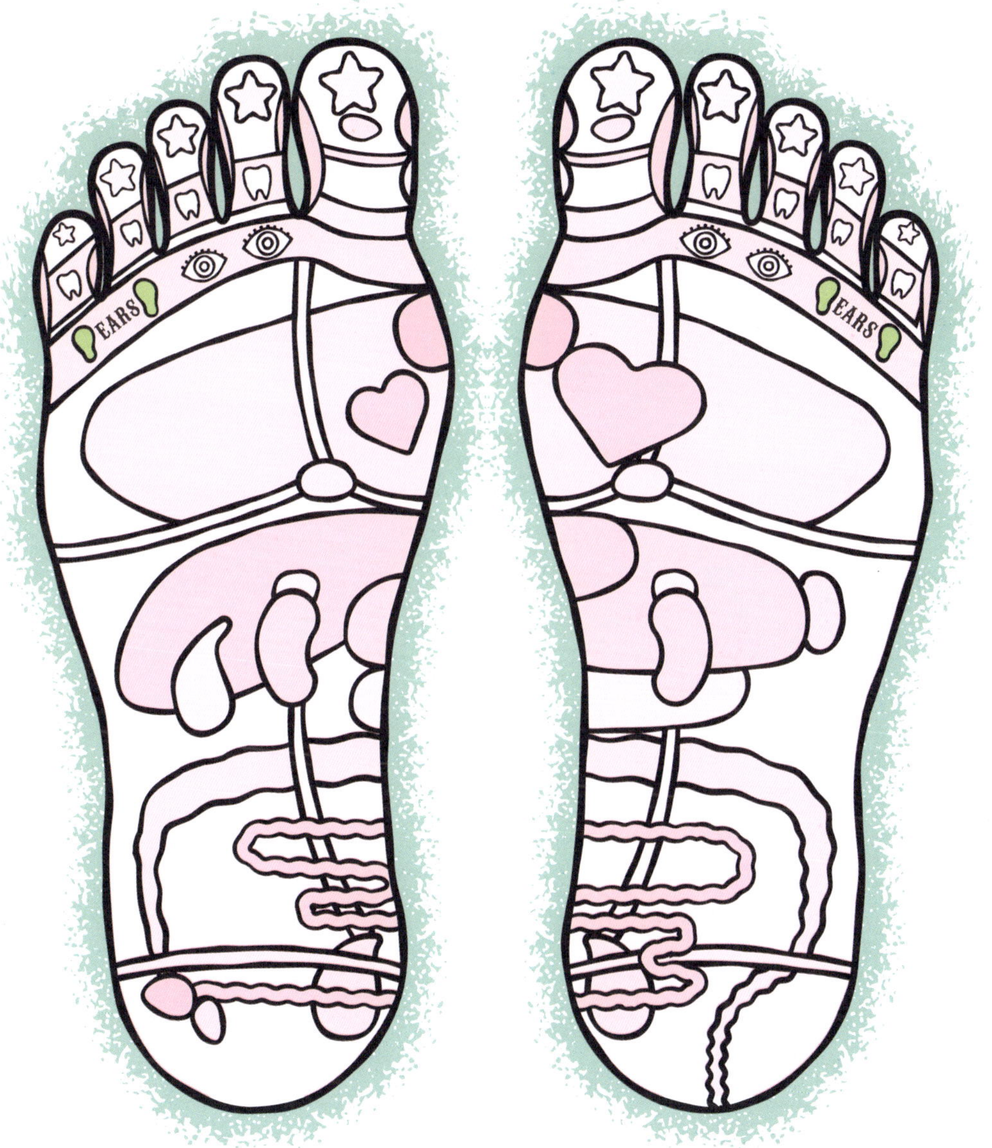

TOES FOR HEAD AND NECK

SHOULDER

The shoulder reflex is located directly below all toes of both feet.

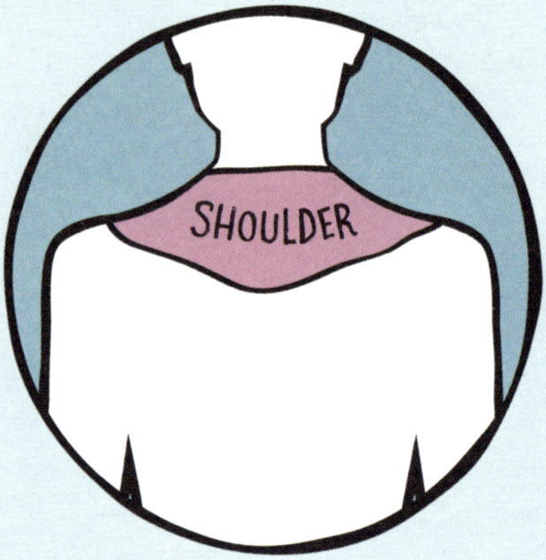

How to work the reflex

If you are experiencing discomfort in one shoulder, begin by working the shoulder reflex of the corresponding foot. Place the pad of your thumb at the inner edge of the foot, directly below the big toe. Using your thumb roll, work all the way across to the outer edge of the foot. Make sure to work close to the toes. You can alternate the directions, working one pass from inner to outer edge, and the next pass from outer to inner edge of the foot. Continue working the upper part of the pad and ball.

If you feel any extra thickness in the tissue, or if an area is more sensitive, give that specific area some additional attention with lighter pressure, until the tissue softens or the tenderness eases. For additional shoulder reflex work, gently squeeze the little webs between the toes. Apply the same techniques on the shoulder reflex of the other foot.

Benefits of working the reflex

When an individual is stressed, or after long hours of desk work, tension is often held in the top of the shoulders. Working the shoulder reflex can help relax the shoulder muscles, reducing pain and discomfort.

TIP: WORK BOTH FEET

It is advised to work the shoulder reflex on both feet, even if the discomfort is experienced on only one side of the body.

47

REFLEX POINTS

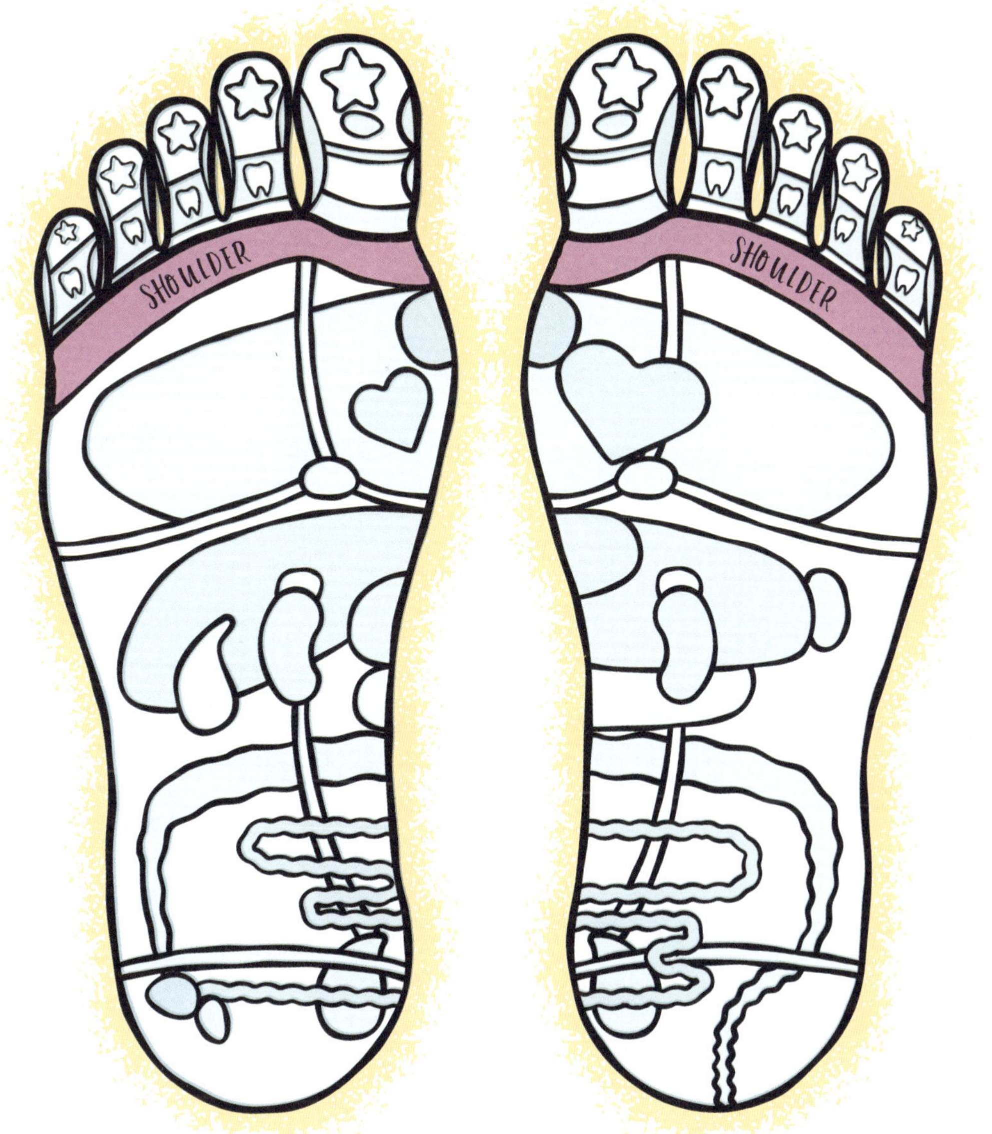

BALL AND PAD FOR CHEST

SHOULDER BLADES

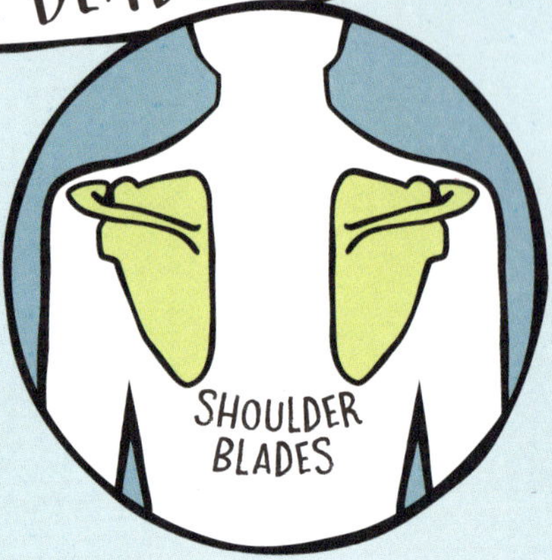

The shoulder blade reflex is located on both feet on the pad below the third and fourth toes. You can also reach the reflex on the top of the feet, in the three outer grooves between the long bones.

How to work the reflex

If you are experiencing discomfort in one shoulder, begin by working the shoulder-blade reflex of the corresponding foot. Place the pad of your thumb directly below the fourth toe and use your thumb-roll technique towards the inner edge until you have covered the area below the fourth and third toes. Lift off your thumb and reflex the area below the fourth and third toes, moving a little closer to the heel with each pass. After you have completed one foot, work the shoulder-blade reflex on the other foot.

Once you have worked on the bottom of both feet, work the three outer grooves between the long bones on top of the feet. Hold the tips of your index, middle and ring fingers next to each other and place them together in the outer groove below the fourth and fifth toes. Hold with gentle pressure for a few minutes, or until any tenderness eases. Repeat the same technique in the grooves below the third and fourth toes, and below the second and third toes. Apply the same technique on the other foot.

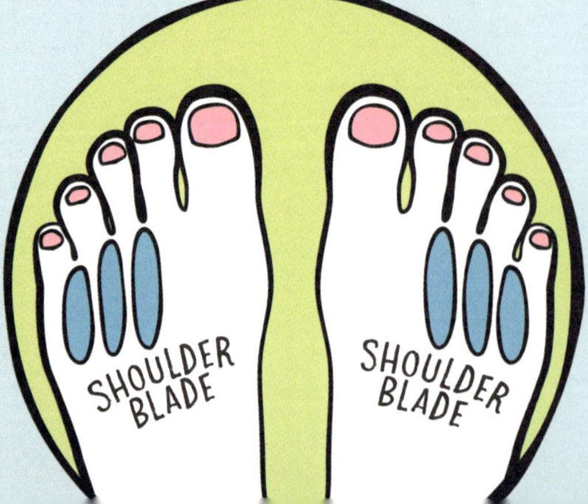

Benefits of working the reflex

The shoulder blade, also called the scapula, is the bone that connects the upper arm with the collar bone. Reflexing the pad on the bottom and the grooves on the top of the feet can help ease pain and discomfort by relaxing the muscles on and around the shoulder blades.

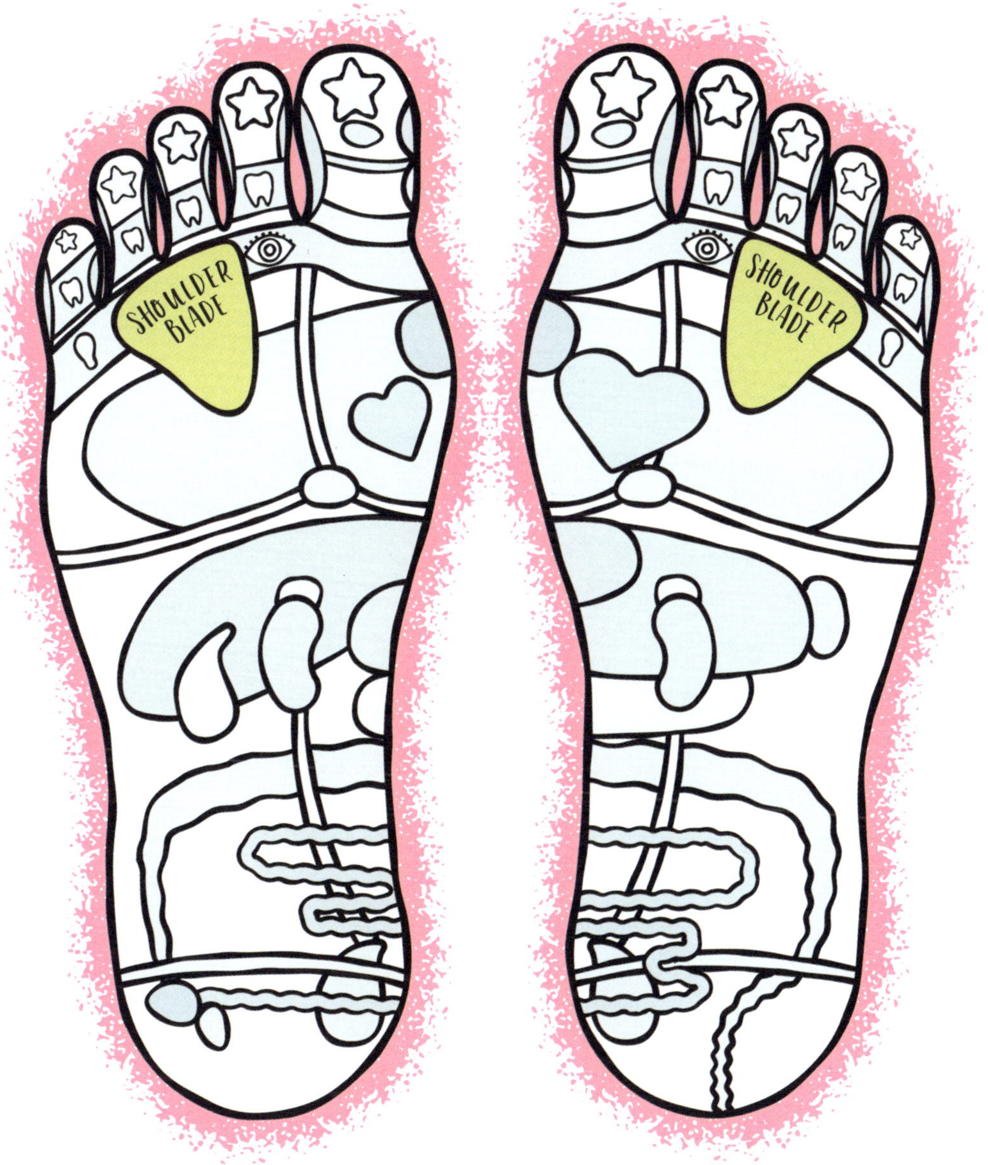

BALL AND PAD FOR CHEST

HEART

The heart reflex is located in the chest region on the ball and pad of both feet. On the left foot, it is below the big and second toes; on the right foot, you'll find it below the big toe.

How to work the reflex

As usual when the reflexes are located on both feet, begin on the left foot. Place the pad of your thumb at the inner edge of the foot, a little below the big toe. Use your thumb-roll technique, working towards the outer edge and reflexing below the big and second toes. Lift off your thumb and start again on the inner edge, a little closer to the heel. Continue until you have covered most of the ball and pad below the toes. After finishing the left foot, work the smaller portion of the heart reflex on the right foot (see reflex diagram, opposite), using the same technique on the ball and pad, below the big toe.

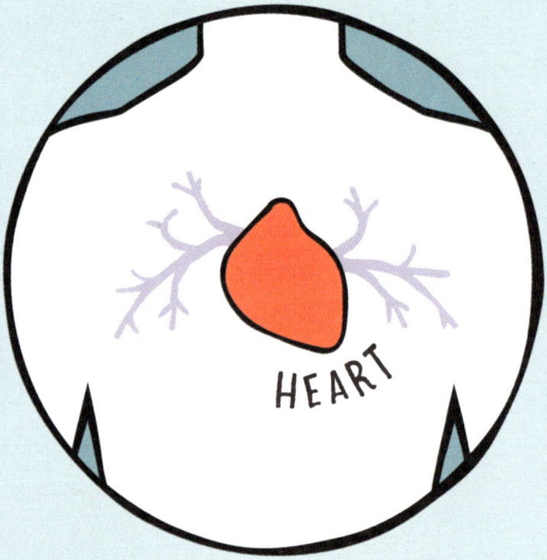

Benefits of working the reflex

Reflexing the ball and pad on the bottom of the feet can help relax the muscles in the entire chest area, where the heart is located. The heart is a specialized muscle, pumping blood throughout the body. When the chest muscles are relaxed and circulation increases in that area, it may help the heart to work more efficiently, thereby minimizing unnecessary strain and stress.

TIP: SOOTHE THE HEART

Work the heart reflex with comforting and soothing thumb-roll pressure and, as always, lighten up if experiencing any tenderness.

51
REFLEX POINTS

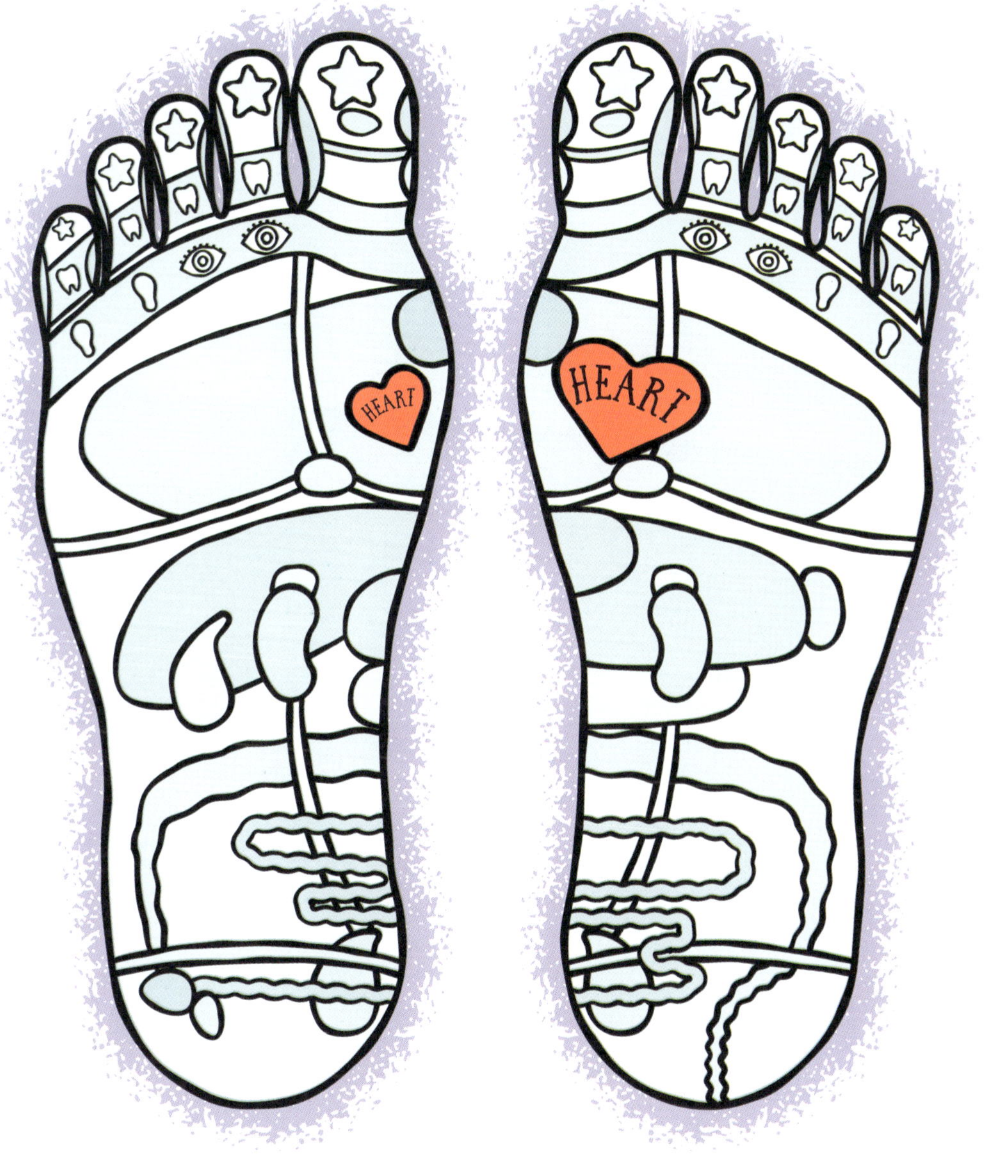

BALL AND PAD FOR CHEST

LUNGS

The lung reflex is located on the ball and pad of both feet, covering most of the chest reflex area. The left lung corresponds to the left foot and vice versa. You can also reach the lung reflex in the four grooves between the long bones on the top of the feet.

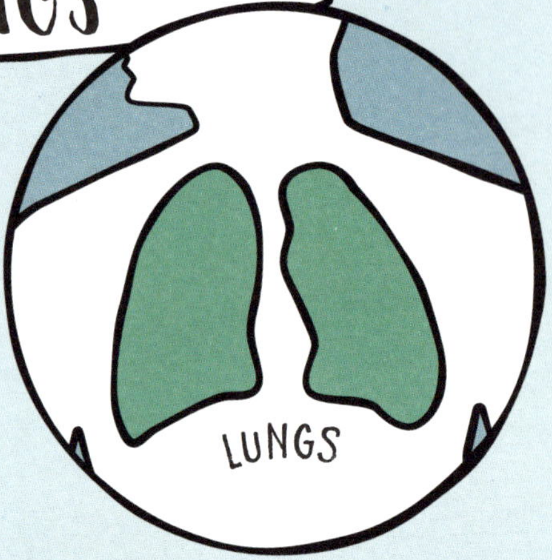

How to work the reflex

Start on the left foot by placing the pad of your thumb at the outer edge of the foot, below the toes, and apply the thumb-roll technique towards the inner edge. Once you reach the inner edge, start again at the outer edge, a little closer to the heel. Continue until you have covered the entire ball and pad of the foot. Work the right foot in the same area using the same technique.

Once you have completed the bottom of both feet, work the grooves between the long bones on the top of the feet. Hold the tips of your index, middle and ring fingers next to each other and place them in the first groove, below the big and second toes of the left foot. Hold with gentle pressure for a few minutes or until any tenderness eases off. Repeat the same technique in the three remaining grooves. Apply the same technique to the right foot.

Benefits of working the reflex

The lungs are part of the respiratory system and allow the exchange of oxygen from the air for carbon dioxide from the body. Reflexing the ball and pad on the bottom and the grooves on top of the feet can help to relax the chest muscles. When the chest muscles are relaxed, circulation increases in that area, improving cell function and helping the lungs to work efficiently.

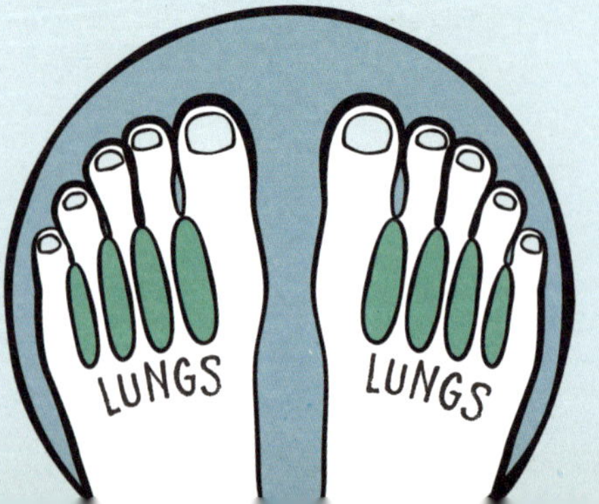

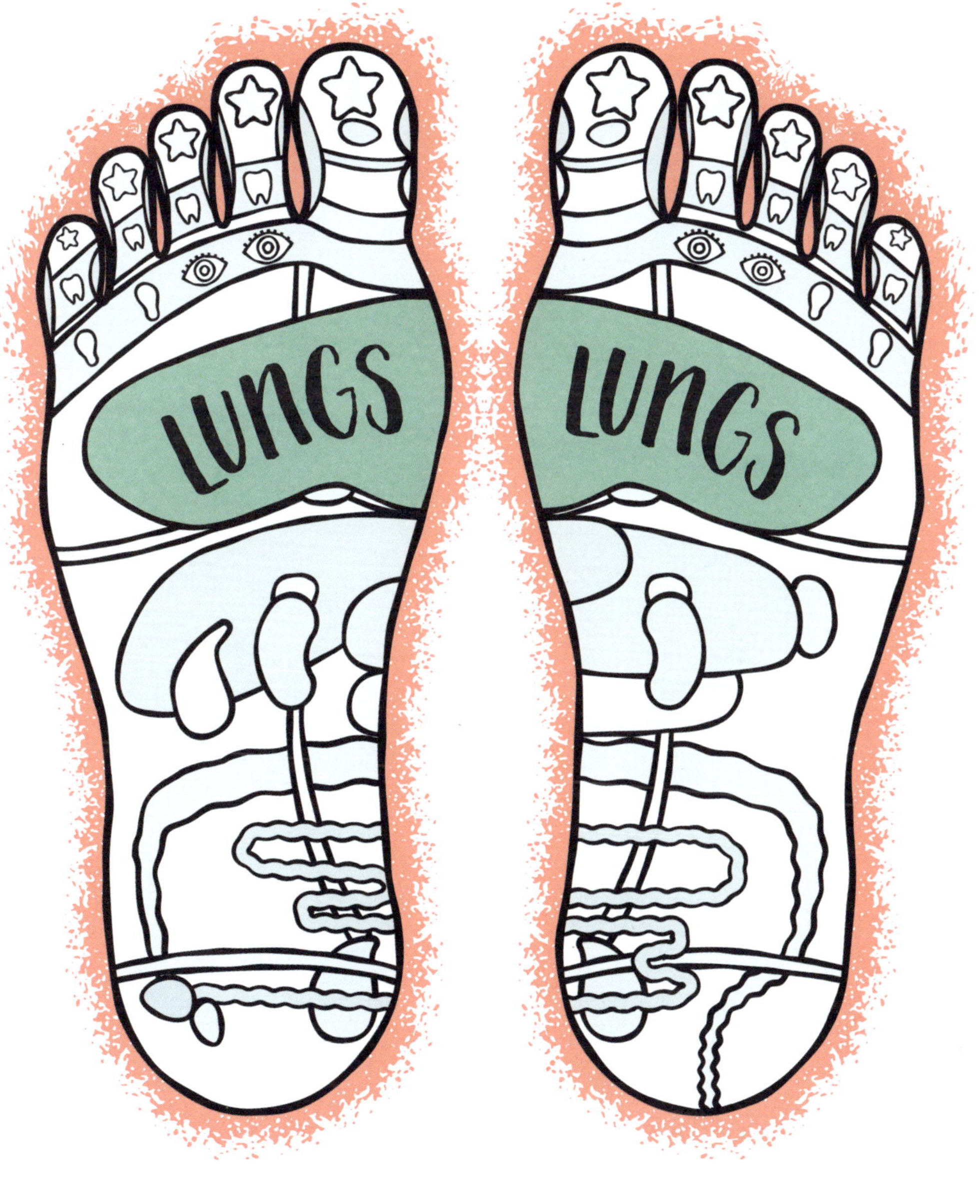

BALL AND PAD FOR CHEST

OESOPHAGUS

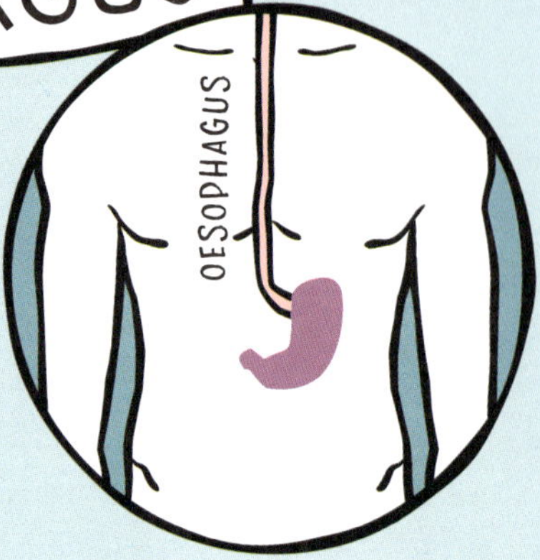

The oesophagus reflex is located on the ball and pad of both feet, starting directly below the toes, between the big toe and second toe, and ending at the diaphragm line.

How to work the reflex

The oesophagus reflex can be worked horizontally as well as vertically. Begin by working horizontally on the left foot by placing the pad of your thumb directly below the big toe. Apply your thumb roll towards the outer edge until you have covered the area below the big and second toe. Lift off your thumb and start again below the big toe a little closer to the heel; continue working until you have reached the upper soft sole at the diaphragm line. Change direction and work the same area between the toes and soft sole towards the inner edge. After you have completed the oesophagus reflex horizontally, you can start to work vertically. Place the pad of your thumb directly below and between the big toe and the second toe. Start your thumb roll towards the heel until you have reached the upper soft sole. Repeat both techniques in the same area on the right foot.

Benefits of working the reflex

The oesophagus is a muscular tube that connects the throat to the stomach. Working the oesophagus reflex may help ease irritation from acid reflux by relaxing the muscles and soothing the nerves that correspond to the oesophagus.

TIP: WORK EVENLY

Use even thumb-roll pressure on the oesophagus reflex to soften the tissue and lighten up if any areas are more sensitive.

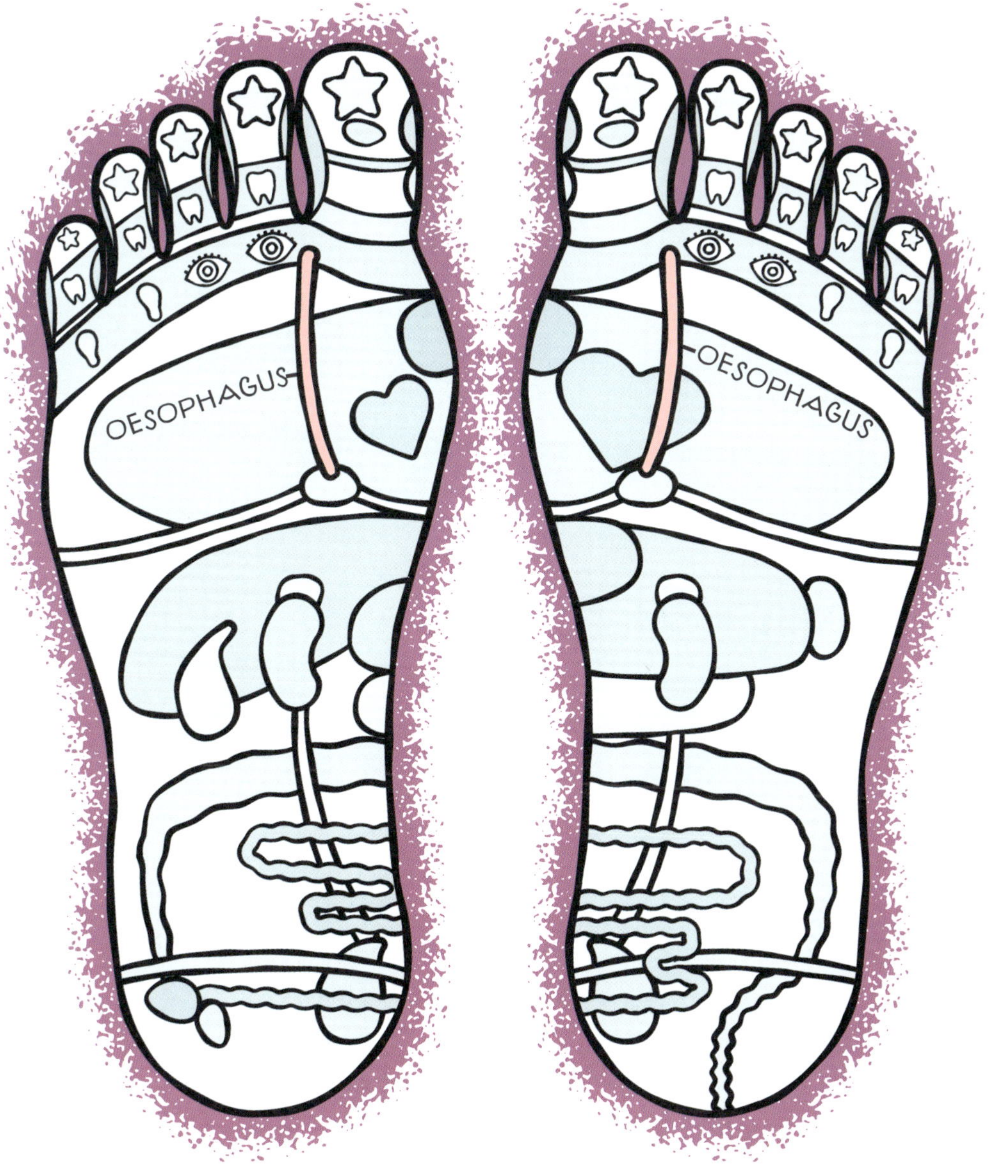

BALL AND PAD FOR CHEST

THYMUS

The thymus reflex is located in the chest region on the ball of both feet, below the big toes.

How to work the reflex

Place the pad of your thumb at the inner edge of the ball of the left foot, below the big toe. Apply your thumb-roll technique towards the outer edge, reflexing the area below the big toe. Lift off your thumb and start again at the inner edge, a little closer to the heel. Continue until you have covered the upper part of the ball below the big toe. After reflexing the left foot, work the right foot with the same technique and in the same area.

Benefits of working the reflex

The thymus is part of the immune system, acting like a training centre for special types of white blood cells and defending the body from invading pathogens. Working the thymus reflex may encourage the body's self-healing ability by improving the immune system.

TIP: ESTABLISH A RHYTHM

Use a slow, rhythmical thumb roll when working the thymus reflex.

57

REFLEX POINTS

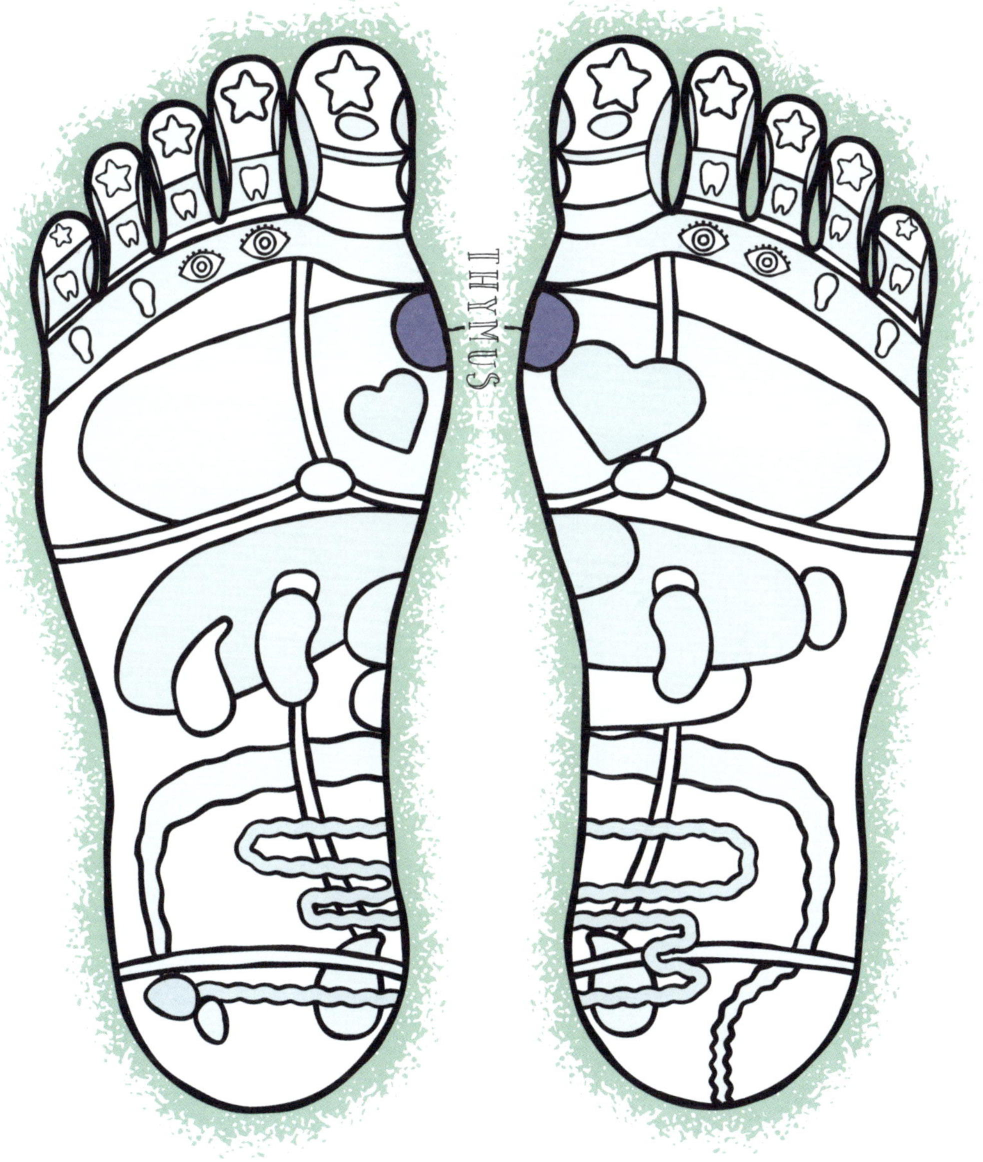

BALL AND PAD FOR CHEST

Breast

The breast reflex is located on the top of the feet, in the four grooves between the long bones.

How to work the reflex

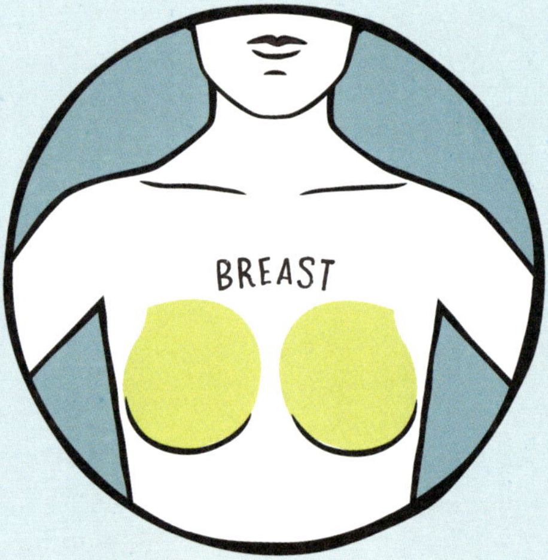

Begin in the grooves of the left foot. Hold the tips of your index, middle and ring fingers next to each other, and place them together in the first groove below the big toe and second toe. Hold with gentle pressure for a few minutes or until any tenderness eases. If the breast reflex is not too sensitive, stretch the skin up towards the toes with your three fingers in the groove, applying very light pressure. Then press gently into the tissue and stretch the skin down towards the leg, maintaining the same gentle pressure. Repeat the same techniques in the three remaining grooves. After working the left foot, repeat on the right foot.

Benefits of working the reflex

Working the breast reflex can help relieve any tenderness that may be felt in the breast. It can also assist in lactation for new mothers.

TIP: SENSITIVE GROOVES

Apply gentle pressure, easing off if the area is tender, as the grooves on top of the feet can be very sensitive.

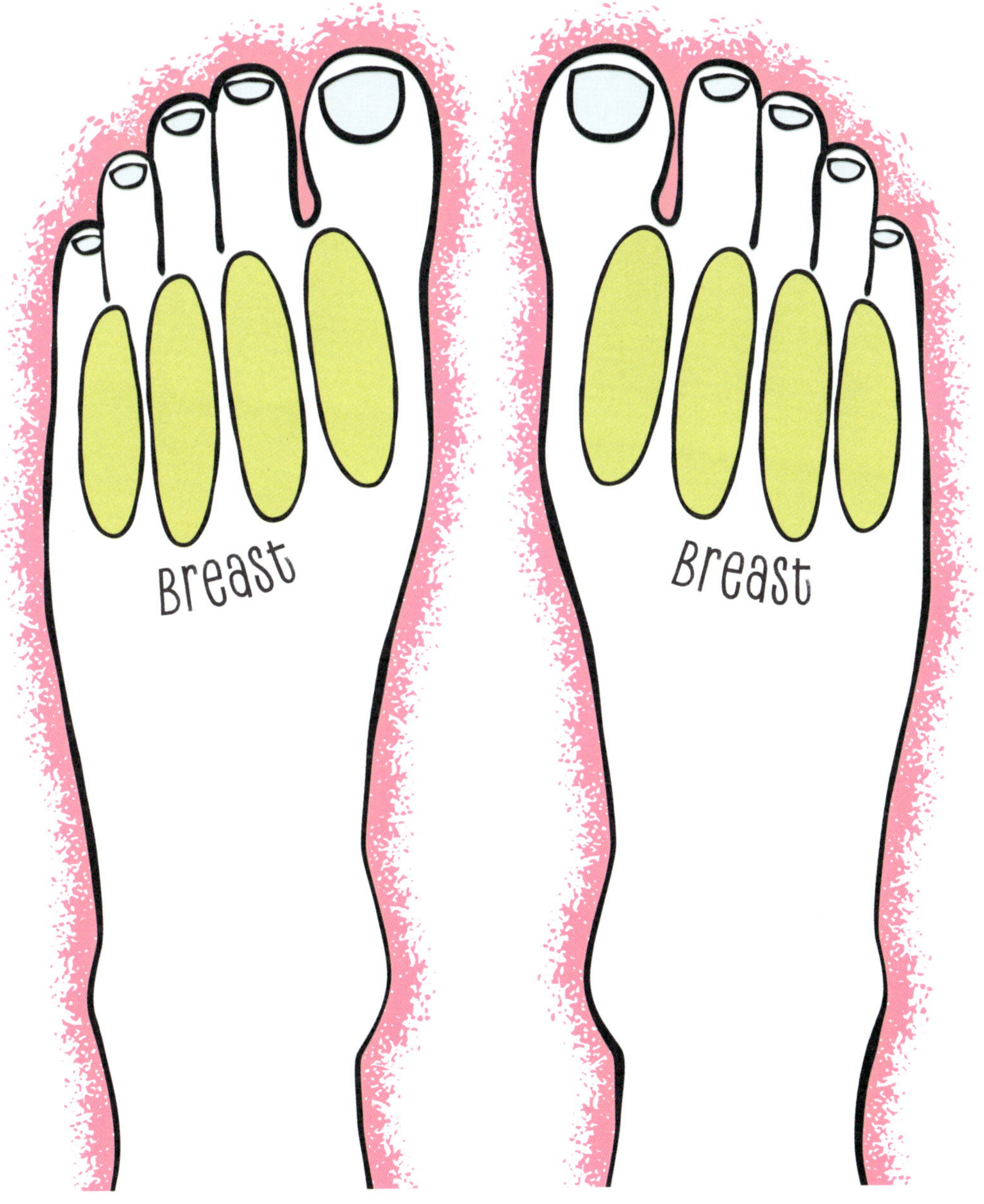

BALL AND PAD FOR CHEST

DIAPHRAGM

The diaphragm reflex is a line running from the inner edge to the outer edge of the feet, located between the ball and pad and the soft sole.

How to work the reflex

Beginning with the left foot, place the pad of your thumb at the inner edge of the foot, just below the ball, and apply the thumb-roll technique all the way to the outer edge. Work in this direction several times across the foot before changing direction, working now from the outer edge to the inner edge several times. Once finished, switch to the right foot and repeat. Work the diaphragm reflex slowly, with gentle and even pressure.

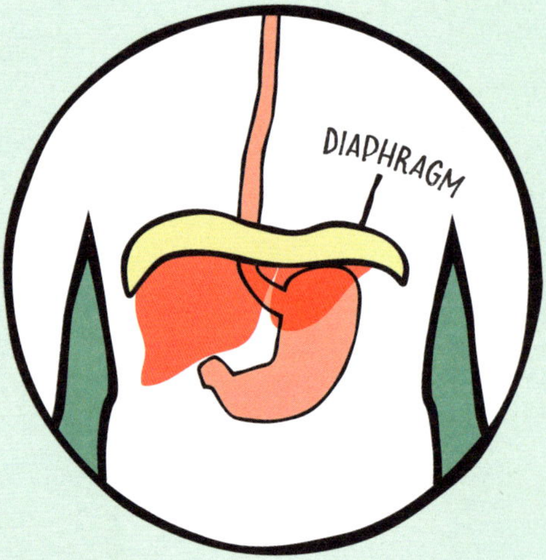

Benefits of working the reflex

The diaphragm is the main muscle of respiration and, as such, is vital to the breathing process. Relaxing the diaphragm may enable you to take deeper breaths, which will supply the body with more oxygen and help to empty the lungs more efficiently. A relaxed diaphragm has a good range of motion, and can also help to stimulate structures, such as the lungs, in the lower chest and stomach, liver and upper abdomen.

TIP: WATCH THE INNER EDGE

Be aware that the area at the inner edge can be sensitive because of anatomical reasons of the foot. As always, when you find tender areas, make sure to lighten up your thumb roll and stay within the pain threshold.

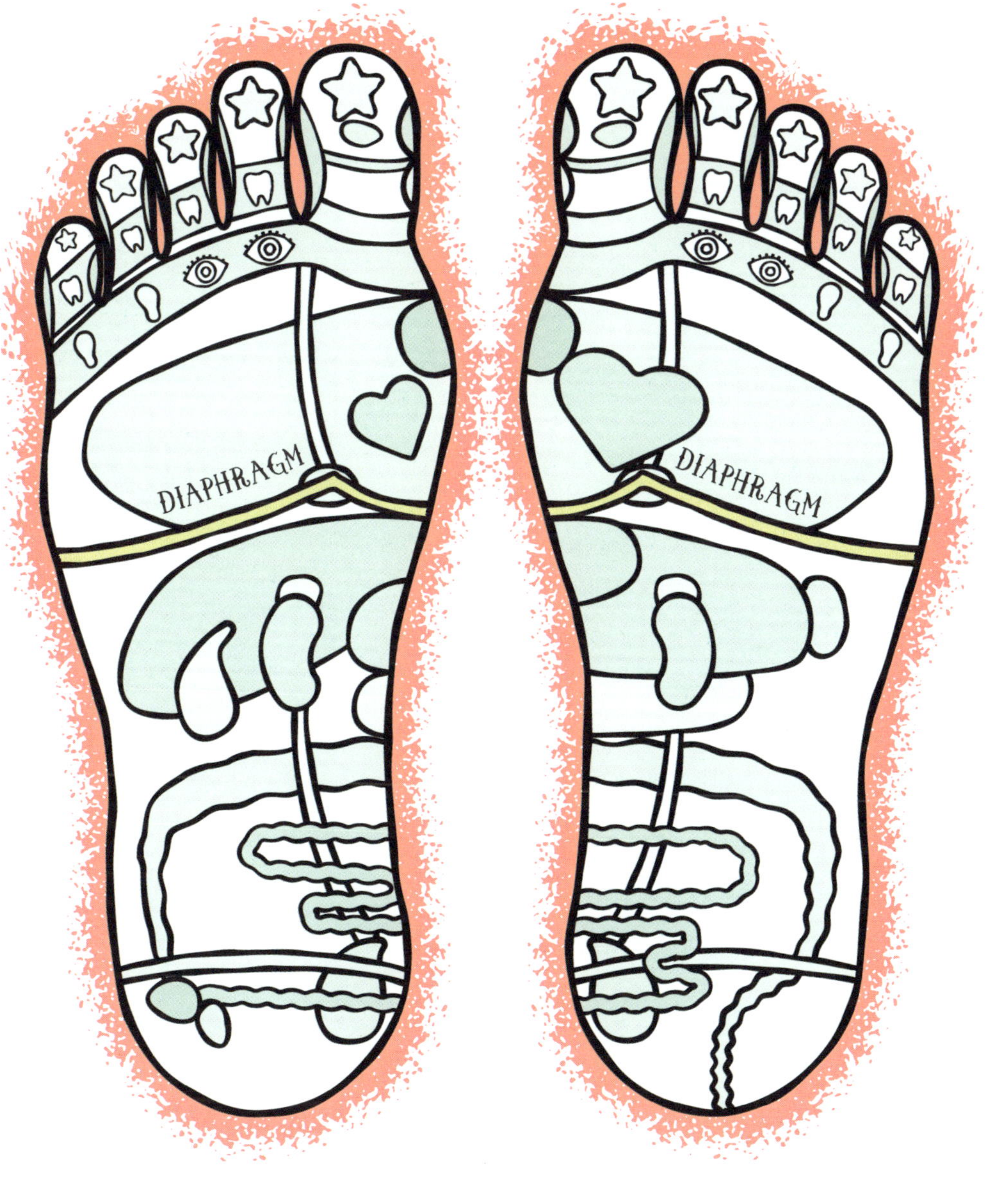

SOFT SOLE FOR UPPER AND MID ABDOMEN

SOLAR PLEXUS

The solar plexus reflex is located on the upper soft sole, directly below the diaphragm line, between the big and second toes of both feet.

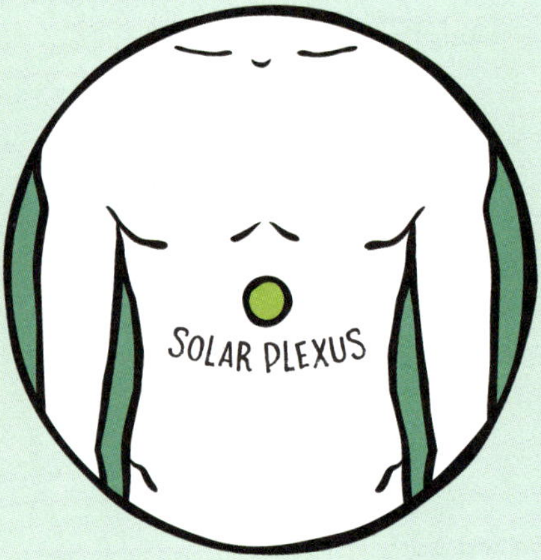

How to work the reflex

Hold the solar plexus reflex on the left foot for a couple of minutes before starting slow and gentle circular movements. As the solar plexus is a nerve cluster, it is important to work the surrounding area as well. Place the pad of your thumb on the diaphragm line below the big toe and work towards the outer edge. Apply a few slow and soothing thumb rolls in the upper soft sole, below the big and second toes. End by holding the solar plexus reflex with your thumb again. Repeat the same sequence on the right foot.

TIP: KEEP IT LIGHT

Make sure to use light pressure. All of the techniques you are using on the solar plexus reflex should be slow and comforting.

Benefits of working the reflex

The solar plexus, also called the celiac ganglion, is a cluster of nerves in the upper abdomen. Releasing tension in the solar plexus by soothing the nerves can help everything in the upper and mid abdomen to work effectively.

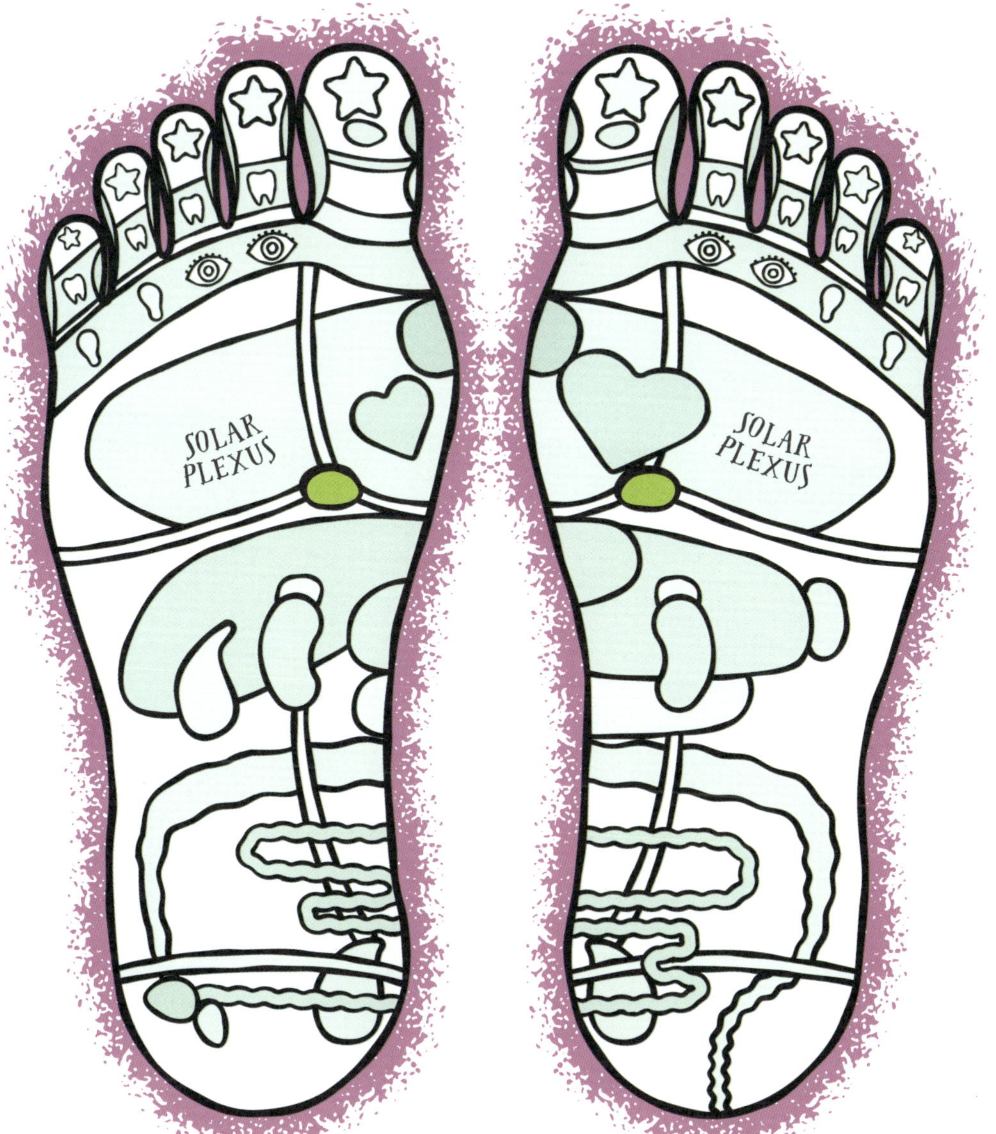

SOFT SOLE FOR UPPER AND MID ABDOMEN

Stomach

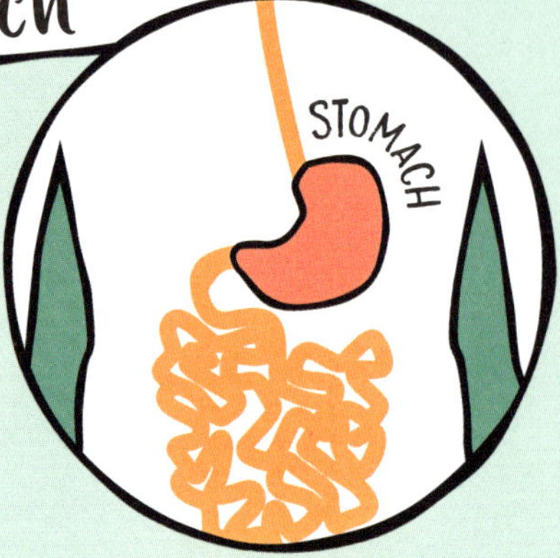

The greater part of the stomach reflex is located on the upper soft sole of the left foot, and a smaller portion on the upper soft sole of the right foot.

How to work the reflex

Begin reflexing the left foot by placing the pad of your thumb at the inner edge of the foot, just below the ball. Start the thumb-roll technique towards the outer edge, until you have covered about two-thirds of the foot's width. Lift off your thumb and start again at the inner edge, just a little closer to the heel than before. Continue this way until you have covered most of the upper soft sole. After completing the left foot, reflex the smaller portion on the right foot with the same thumb-roll technique, beginning at the inner edge and working towards the outer edge.

TIP: TAKE IT SLOW

Work slowly with gentle, comforting and even pressure, easing off when you find an area that is more sensitive. Keep reflexing until you feel the tissue underneath the skin becoming softer and the tenderness subsides.

Benefits of working the reflex

The stomach, a hollow, muscular organ, helps digest food by secreting acid and enzymes. Working the stomach reflex can soothe the stomach, ease aches and pains and help the stomach to function at its optimum level.

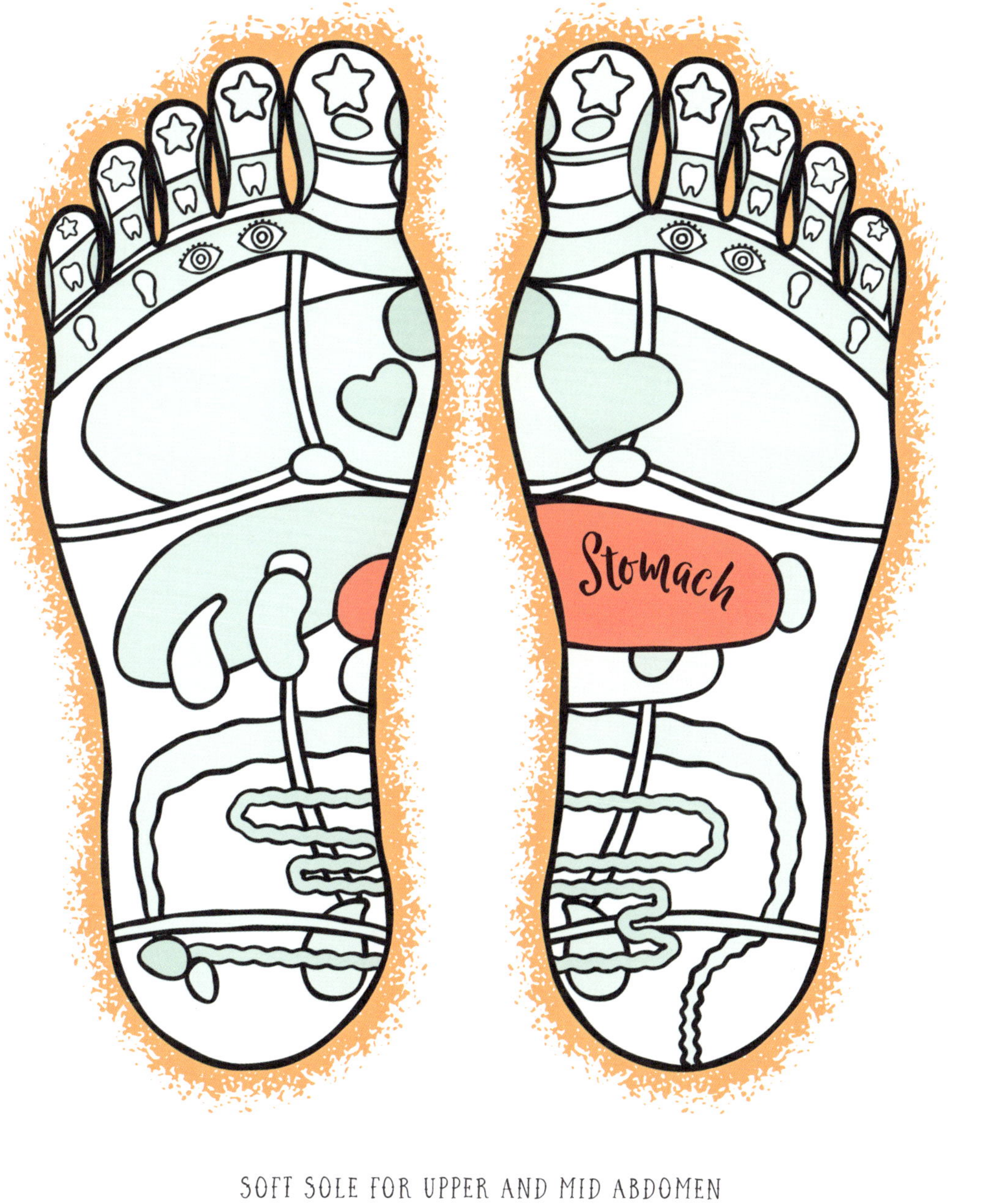

SOFT SOLE FOR UPPER AND MID ABDOMEN

SPLEEN

The spleen reflex is located on the left foot, in the upper soft sole below the fourth toe.

How to work the reflex

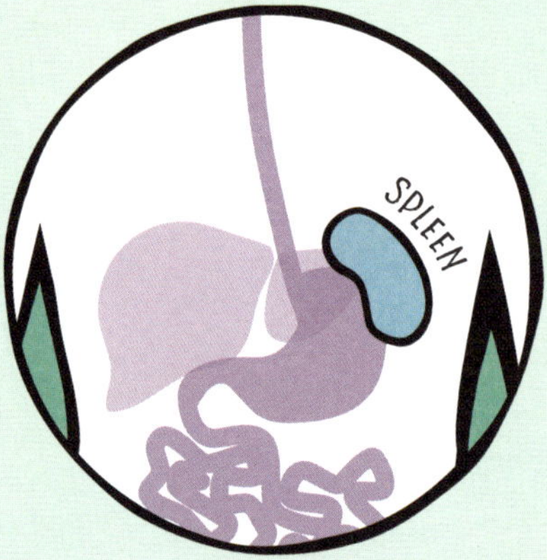

Place your thumb on the upper soft sole, halfway between the inner and outer edge of the foot. Begin your thumb-roll technique towards the outer edge, until you have covered the area of the soft sole below the fourth toe. Lift off your thumb and work the same area, just a little closer to the heel, and continue until you have covered most of the outer upper soft sole.

Hold any sensitive area with the pad of your thumb until tenderness eases off, and continue reflexing with lighter pressure.

Benefits of working the reflex

The spleen purifies the blood and helps to fight infections, playing an important role in the immune system. Working the spleen reflex may encourage the spleen to function well and improve the immune system.

TIP: TEND TO THE WIDER AREA

Every person is different, so it is advised to work the broader area, as described above, to ensure that all of the spleen reflex is covered.

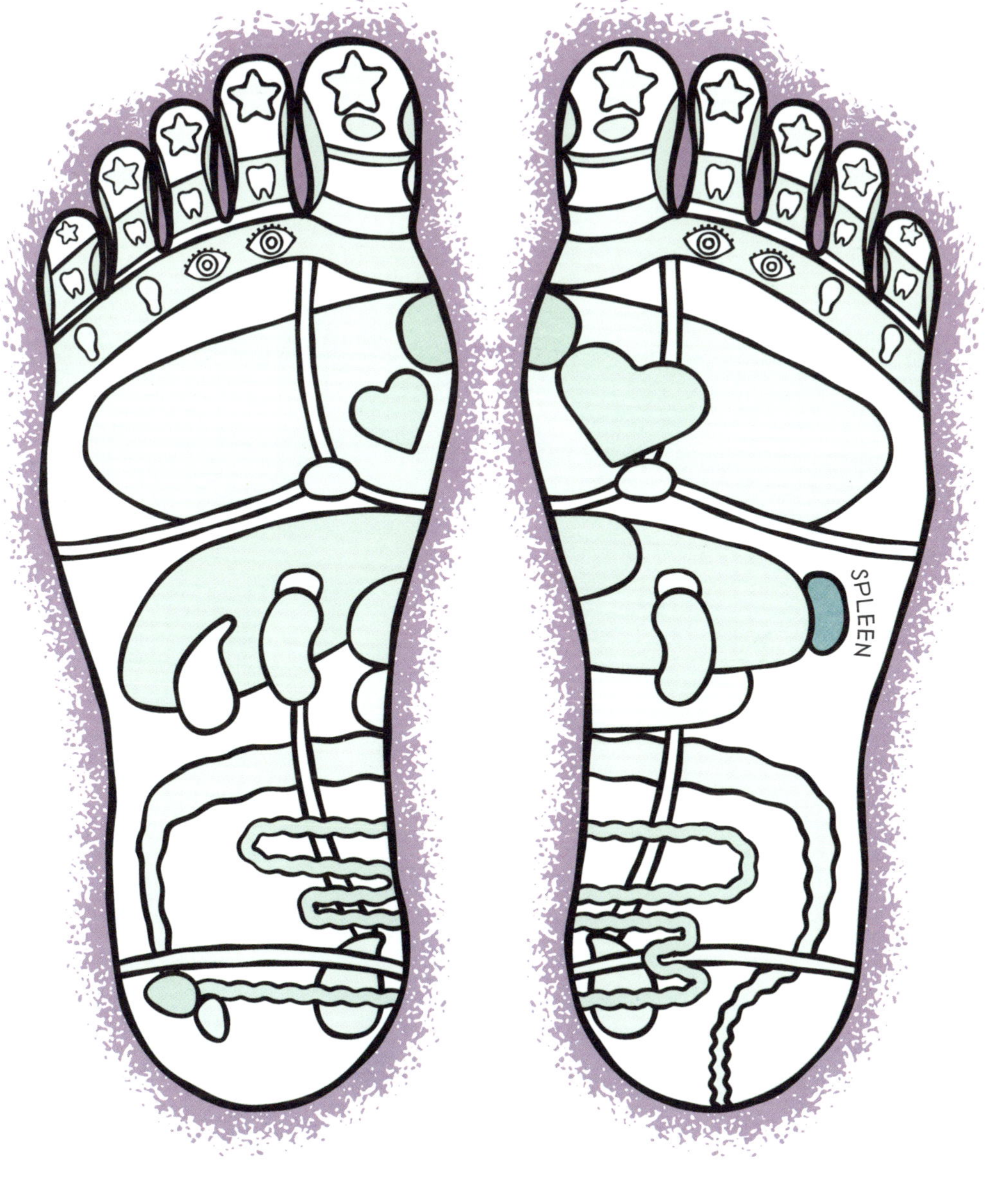

SOFT SOLE FOR UPPER AND MID ABDOMEN

LIVER

The liver reflex is a large area on the soft sole of both feet. The greater portion of the liver reflex is located on the upper and mid soft sole of the right foot, and a smaller portion on the upper soft sole of the left foot.

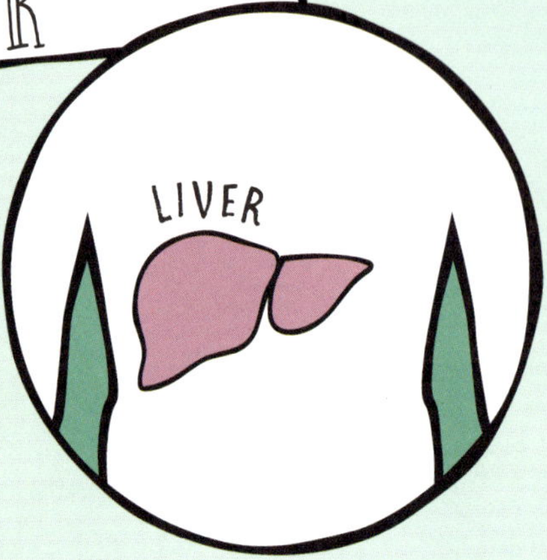

How to work the reflex

Begin reflexing the larger part of the reflex on the right foot by placing the pad of your thumb at the inner edge of the foot, just below the ball. Apply the thumb-roll technique towards the outer edge, until you have covered the whole width of the foot. Lift off your thumb and start again at the inner edge, just a little closer to the heel. Continue until you have covered all of the upper and mid soft sole. Starting at the inner edge, move to the smaller part of the reflex on the left foot by applying the thumb-roll technique towards the outer edge, until you have covered about one third of the foot's width. Continue until you have reflexed most of the upper soft sole for the smaller portion of the liver reflex.

Benefits of working the reflex

The liver is a large filter organ with many vital functions, including filtering harmful substances from blood – such as metabolic waste products, old red blood cells, alcohol and drugs – and playing an important role in fat metabolism. Working the liver reflex can help the liver function at its maximum potential and encourage detoxification.

TIP: SOFTEN THE TISSUE

Work the liver reflex with even and comforting pressure, until you feel the tissue underneath the skin softening. If any areas are particularly sensitive, lighten your thumb-roll pressure until the area becomes less tender.

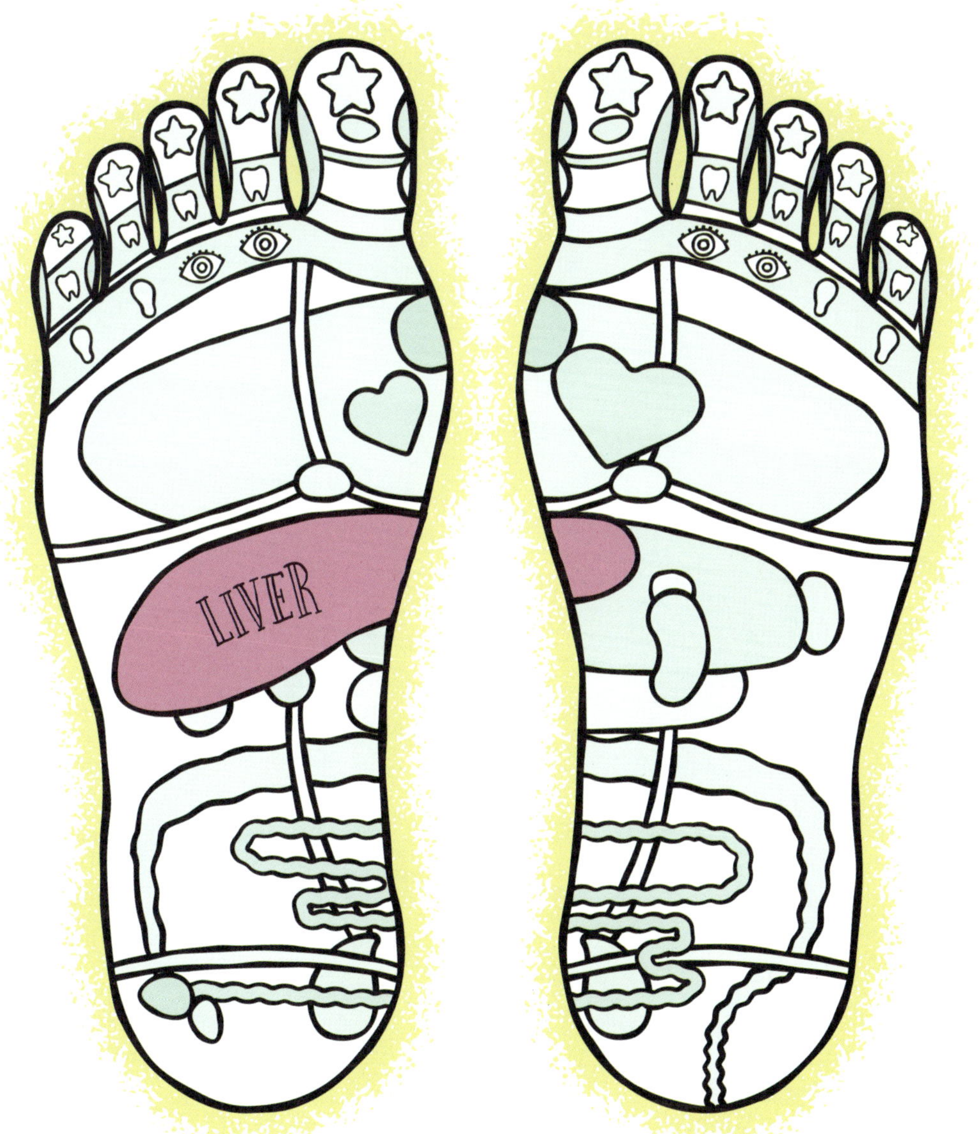

SOFT SOLE FOR UPPER AND MID ABDOMEN

GALLBLADDER

The gallbladder reflex is located on the upper soft sole of the right foot, with the upper half on and the lower half below the liver reflex.

How to work the reflex

Start on the upper soft sole of your right foot, halfway between the inner edge and the outer edge. Applying the thumb-roll technique, work towards the outer edge of the foot. Lift off your thumb and begin again on the same starting point, just a little closer to the heel. Continue in this way until you have covered most of the outer upper soft sole.

Due to its anatomical connections to the liver and the small intestine, it is advisable to also work the area surrounding the gallbladder reflex.

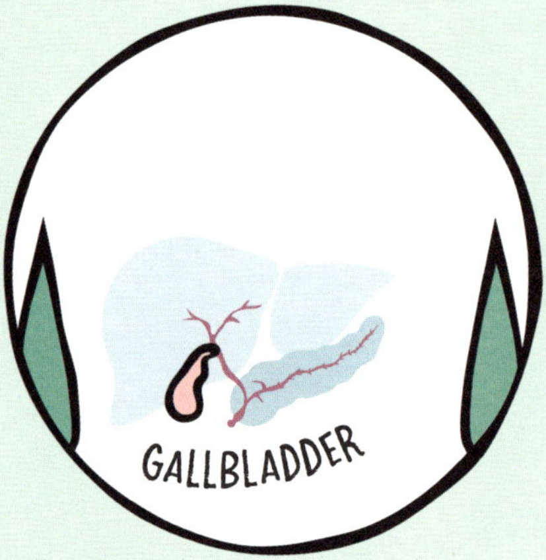

Benefits of working the reflex

The gallbladder is the holding container for bile, which is produced by the liver and helps digest fat from your food. Working the gallbladder reflex may assist in healthy gallbladder functioning.

TIP: HOLD TO EASE

Work with lighter pressure if any area is sensitive. In addition to using the thumb roll, you can hold any tender area with the pad of your thumb until it becomes less sensitive.

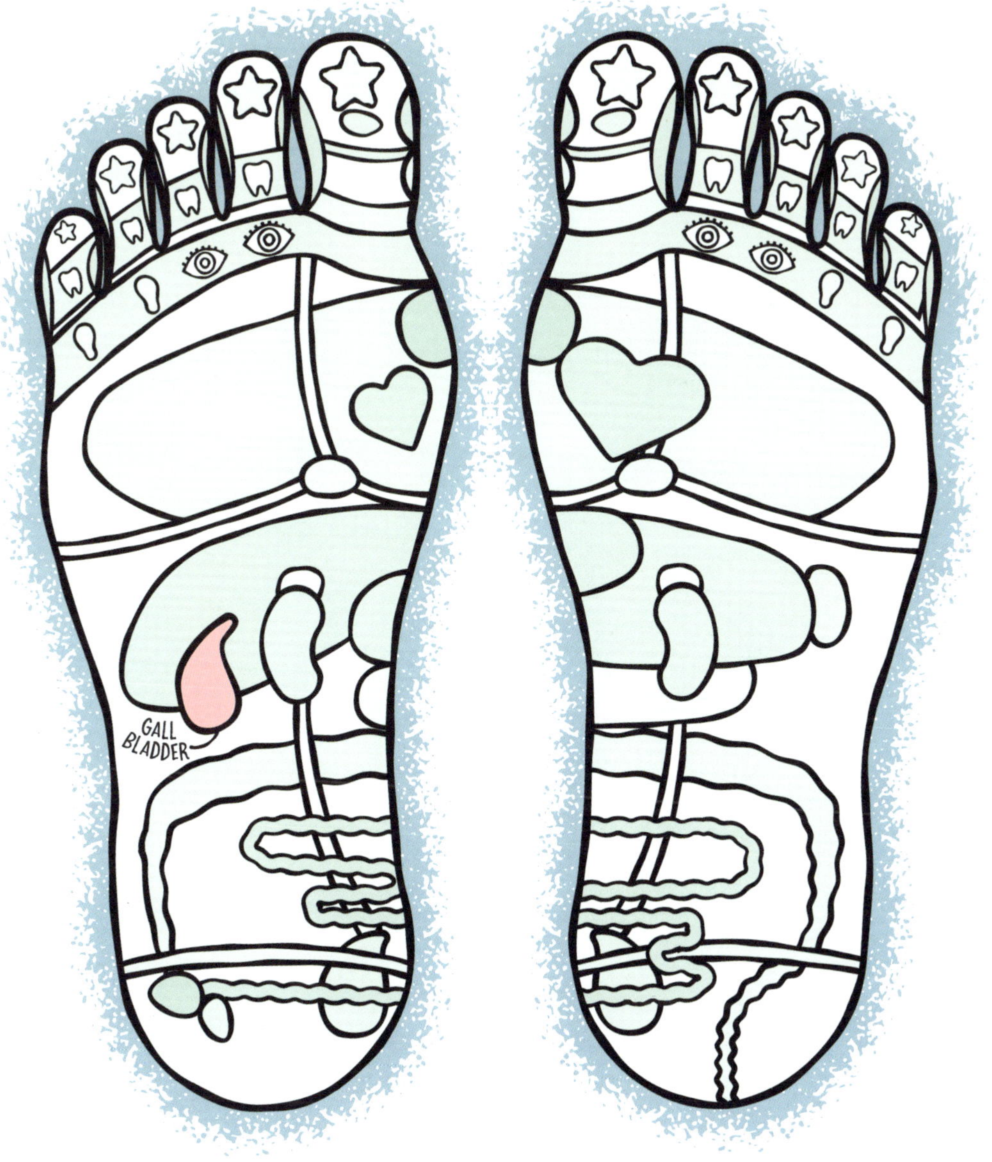

SOFT SOLE FOR UPPER AND MID ABDOMEN

PANCREAS

The greater part of the pancreas reflex is located on the left foot in the mid soft sole, and a smaller portion on the mid soft sole of the right foot.

How to work the reflex

Begin by reflexing the greater part of the pancreas reflex on the left foot. Place the pad of your thumb at the inner edge of the foot, about halfway between the ball and pad and the heel. Start with your thumb-roll technique towards the outer edge of the foot, until you are halfway across. Lift off your thumb and start again at the inner edge, just a little closer to the heel than before.

Continue until you have covered the mid-section of the soft sole. After completing the left foot, start reflexing the smaller part of the pancreas reflex on the right foot, on the mid-section of the soft sole. Begin the thumb roll, again at the inner edge, working below the big toe towards the outer edge. Lift off your thumb and start again, a little closer to the heel, and continue for a few more passes.

Benefits of working the reflex

The pancreas produces digestive juices to help break down food. It also produces insulin to regulate the body's blood-sugar level. Soothing the nerve endings in the pancreas reflex area may help the pancreas function at its optimum, while improving digestion and blood-sugar levels.

TIP: SPEND TIME ON THE LEFT

Because most of the pancreas is on the left side of the body, you should spend more time working the left foot.

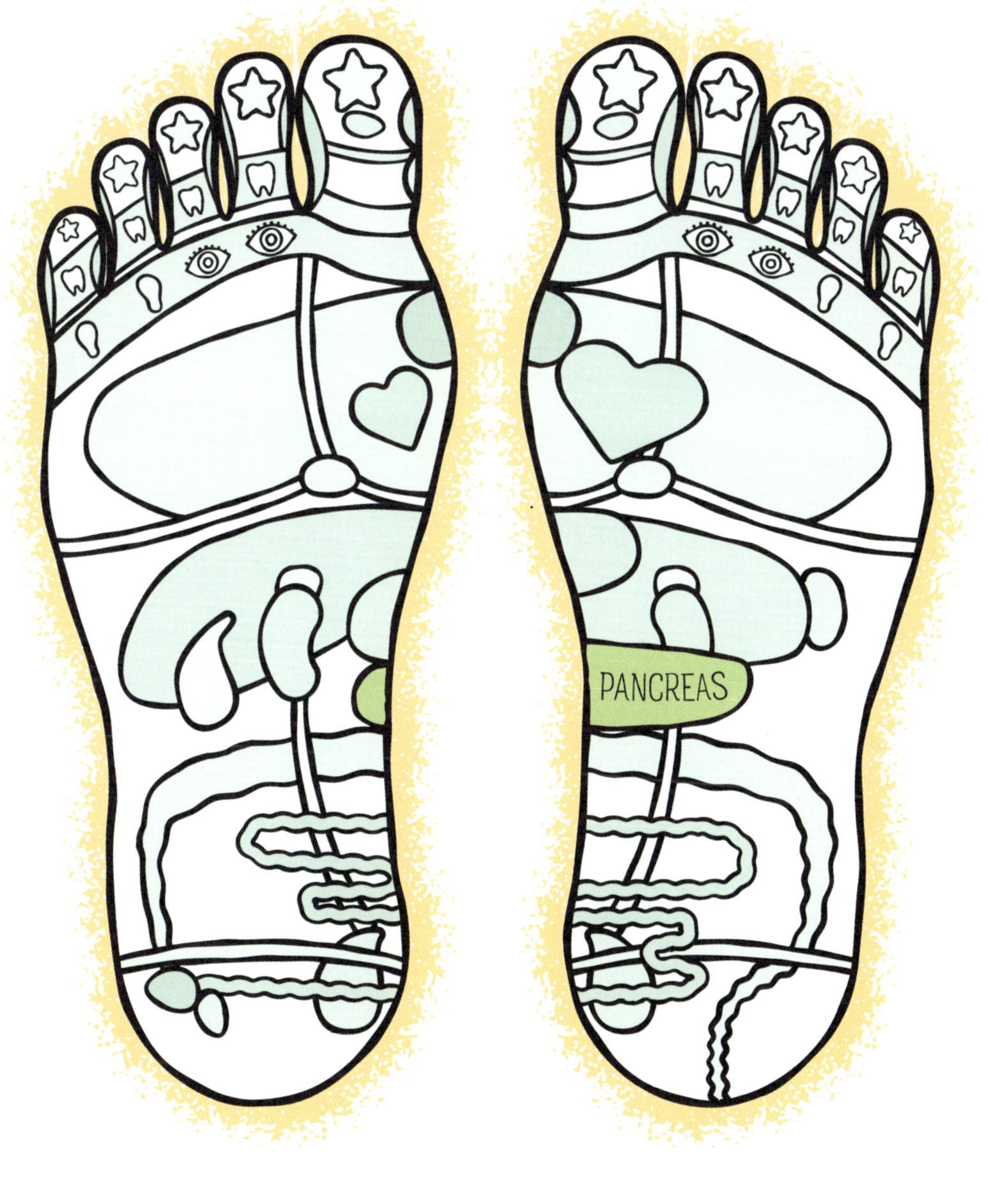

SOFT SOLE FOR UPPER AND MID ABDOMEN

ADRENAL GLANDS

The adrenal gland reflex is a small area located on the upper soft sole of both feet, below the second toe, sitting directly above the kidney reflex (see pages 76–77).

How to work the reflex

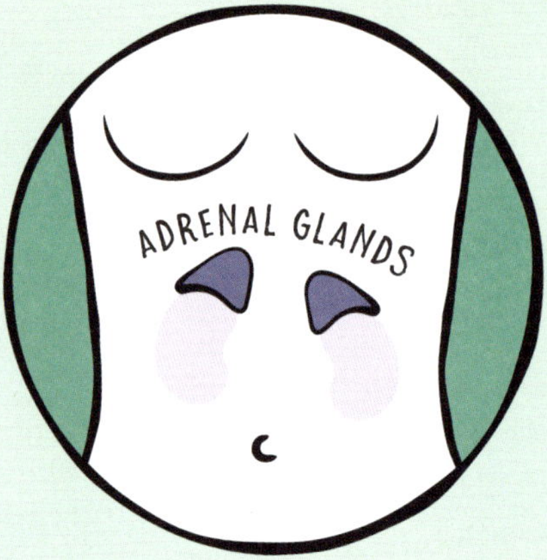

Begin by placing the pad of your thumb on the upper soft sole of the left foot, between the big toe and second toe. Work the adrenal gland reflex with your thumb-roll technique towards the outer edge, until you have covered the area below the second toe. Lift off your thumb and continue reflexing the same area for a few minutes with gentle pressure. To activate the adrenal gland reflex, place the pad of your thumb directly on the reflex and gently press and release a few times.

For additional work, alternate between the thumb roll and the press-and-release technique. Repeat the same sequence of techniques in the same area on the right foot.

Benefits of working the reflex

The adrenal glands are located above the kidneys. They produce certain stress hormones that help your body react to stress, and play an important role in regulating the immune system. Working the adrenal gland reflexes can help the body deal more efficiently with stress, chronic inflammation, autoimmune diseases, allergies and more.

TIP: EASING TENDERNESS

If the adrenal gland reflex is tender to touch, hold it with the pad of your thumb for a few minutes or until the tenderness eases off.

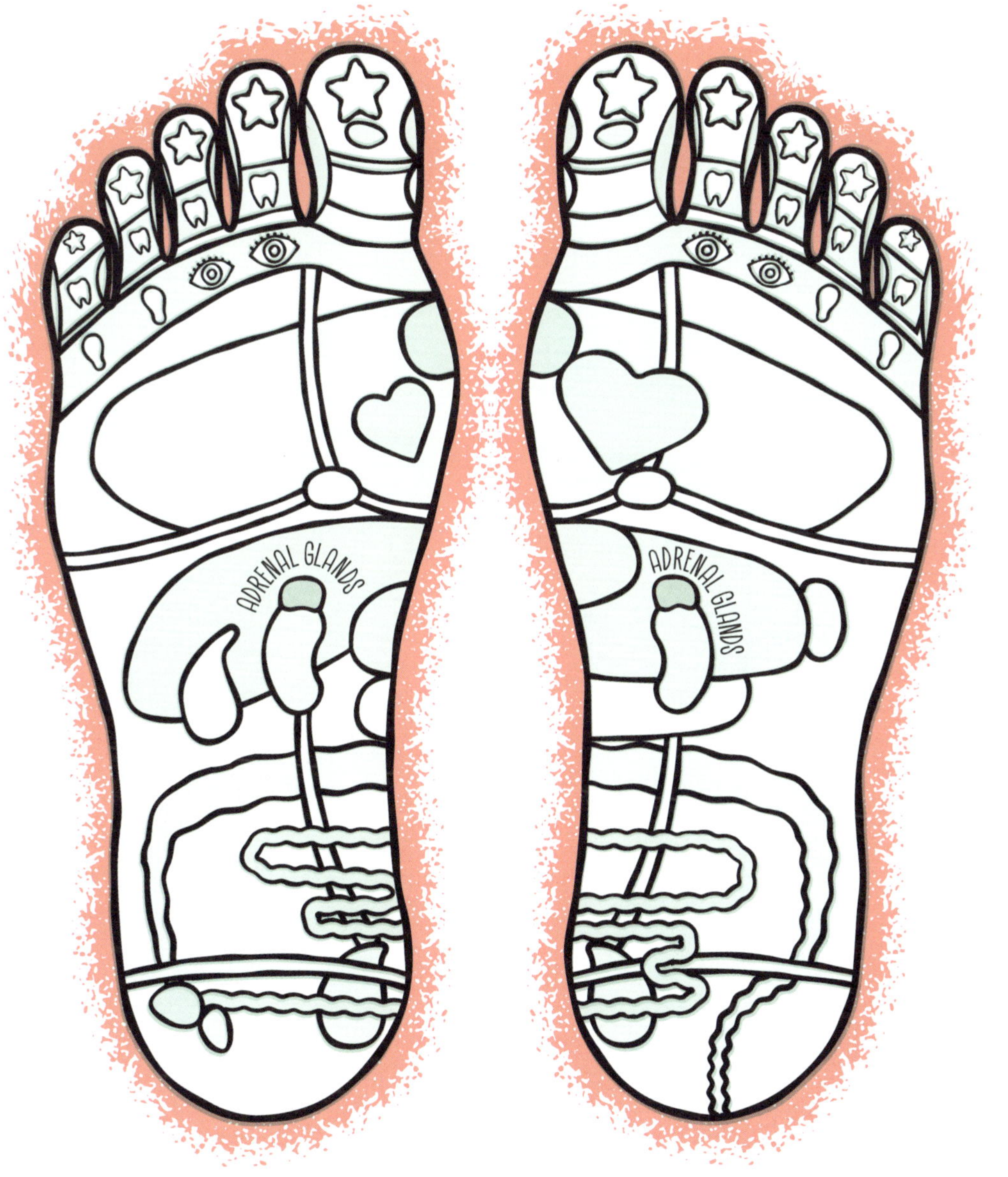

SOFT SOLE FOR UPPER AND MID ABDOMEN

KIDNEYS

The kidney reflex is located on the mid soft sole of both feet below the second toe.

How to work the reflex

Begin working the kidney reflex by placing the pad of your thumb on the mid soft sole of the left foot, between the big and second toes. Apply your thumb-roll technique towards the outer edge, until you have covered the area below the second toe. Lift off your thumb and start again a little closer to the heel, and continue reflexing most of the mid soft sole below the second toe. After you have completed the left foot, repeat the same technique in the same area on the right foot.

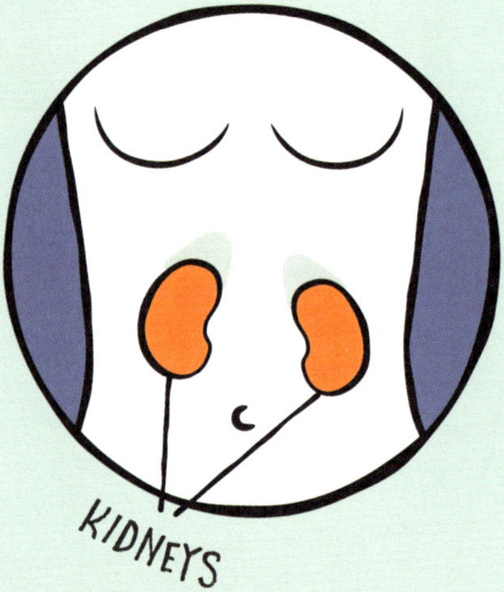

Benefits of working the reflex

The two kidneys in your body filter waste products and extra water from the blood to produce urine. Working the kidney reflex can help to relieve pain and discomfort from kidney infection or kidney stones.

TIP: BEWARE OF TENDONS

Begin with light to medium pressure, as you are reflexing over tendons in this part of the soft sole. Lighten up if any areas are sensitive to touch.

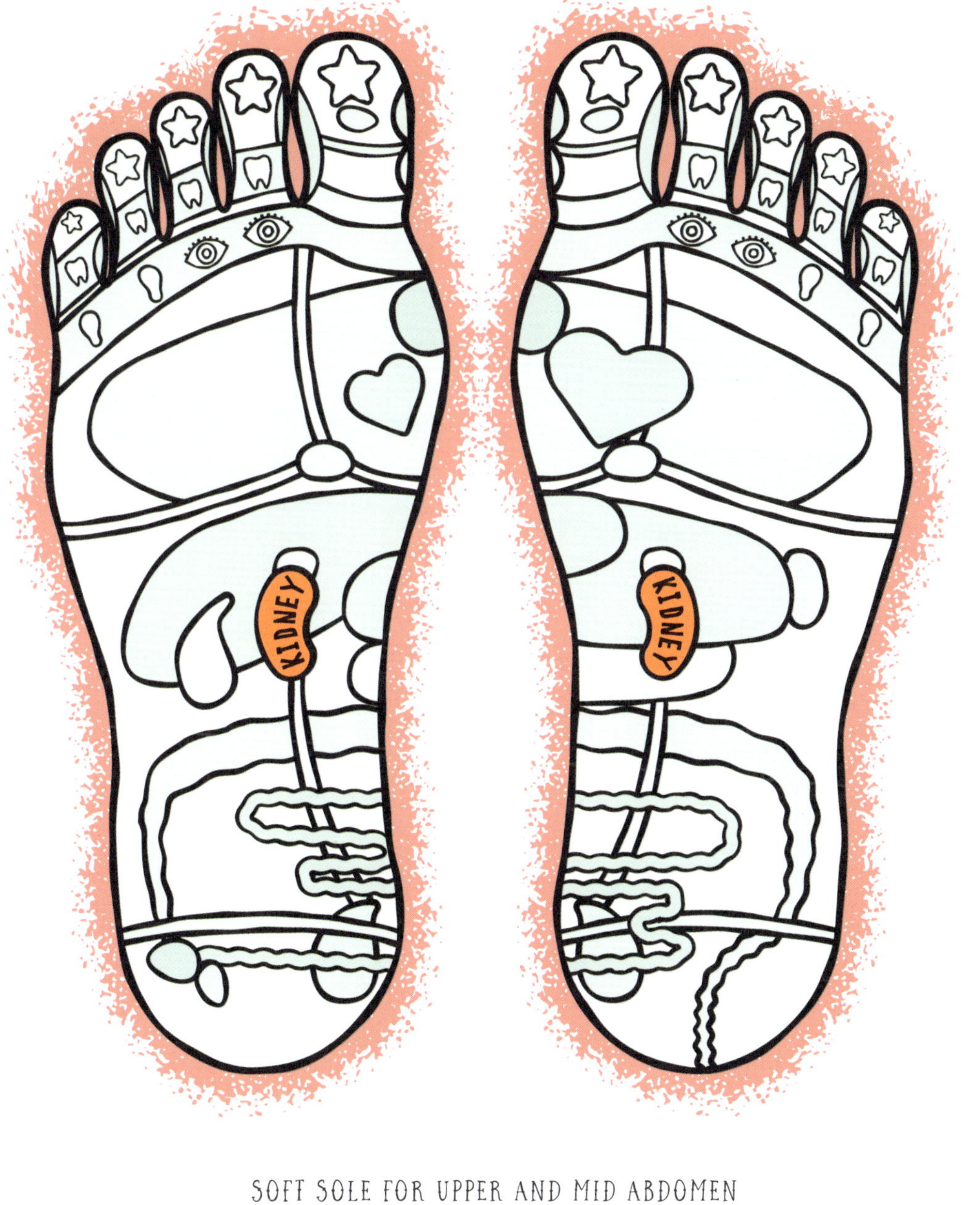

SOFT SOLE FOR UPPER AND MID ABDOMEN

URETERS

The ureter reflex is located on the soft sole of both feet, starting at the kidney reflex (see pages 76–77) in the mid soft sole and ending at the urinary bladder reflex (see pages 92–93) on the heel.

How to work the reflex

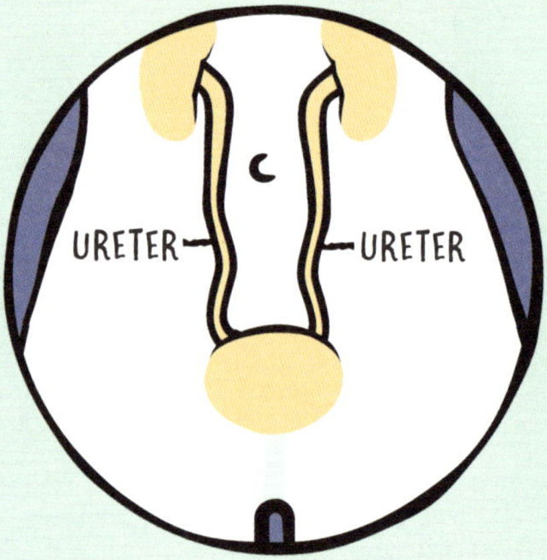

Begin working the ureter reflex horizontally on the left foot by placing the pad of your thumb on the mid soft sole between the big and second toes. Work with your thumb-roll technique towards the outer edge until you have covered the area below the second toe. Lift off your thumb and start again a little closer to the heel. Continue working the soft sole below the big and second toes until you reach the heel. Repeat on the right foot in the same area and with the same thumb-roll technique.

Benefits of working the reflex

There are two ureters in your body – hollow, muscular tubes carrying urine from the kidneys to the urinary bladder. Working the ureter reflex can help relax the muscles in that area of the body, and may assist in keeping the ureters healthy.

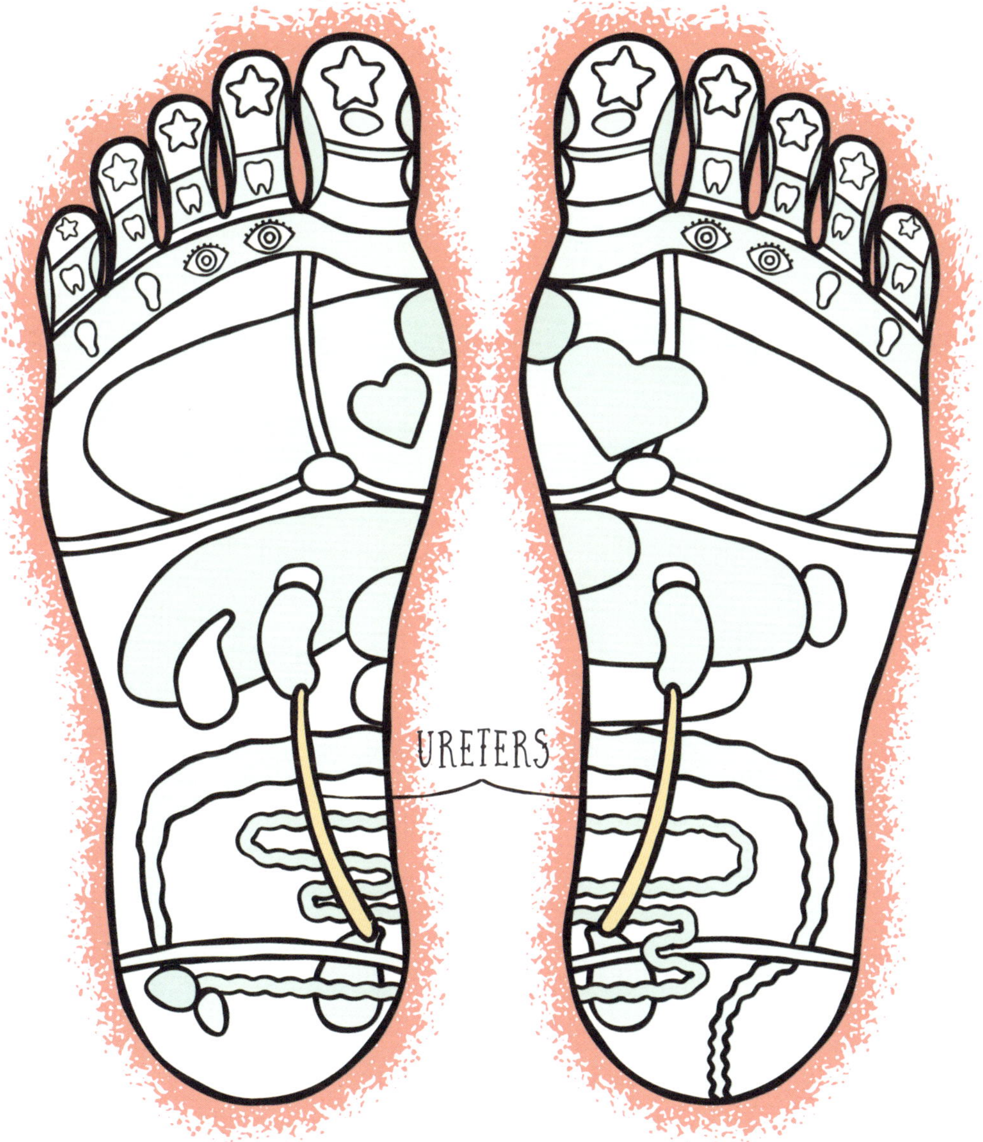

SOFT SOLE FOR UPPER AND MID ABDOMEN

Small Intestine

The small intestine reflex is a large area located on the entire lower soft sole and heel of both feet.

How to work the reflex

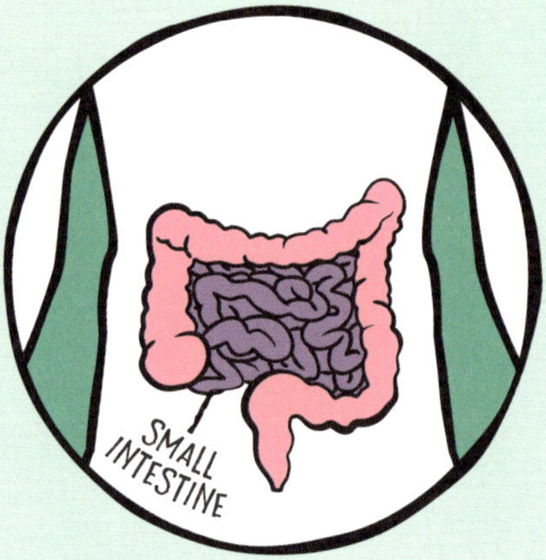

Begin by reflexing the lower soft sole and heel of the left foot. Place the pad of your thumb at the inner edge of the foot, at the lower soft sole, and work with your thumb-roll technique all the way across to the outer edge. Lift off your thumb and start again at the inner edge, just a little closer to the heel, until you have completed reflexing all of the lower soft sole and heel. Repeat on the right foot in the same area and with the same thumb-roll technique.

For best results, work the small intestine reflex slowly and methodically to soften the tissue of the soft sole and heel. If you find any tender or sensitive areas, keep working with lighter pressure until the tenderness eases.

Benefits of working the reflex

The small intestine is a long, winding tube between the stomach and the colon where most of the nutrients from food are absorbed. Because of its key role in digestion, working the small intestine reflex thoroughly may help improve all digestive functions.

TIP: RETURN TO TENDER SPOTS

Revisit any tender area a few more times after completing the soft sole and heel, instead of working the area only once for a long time.

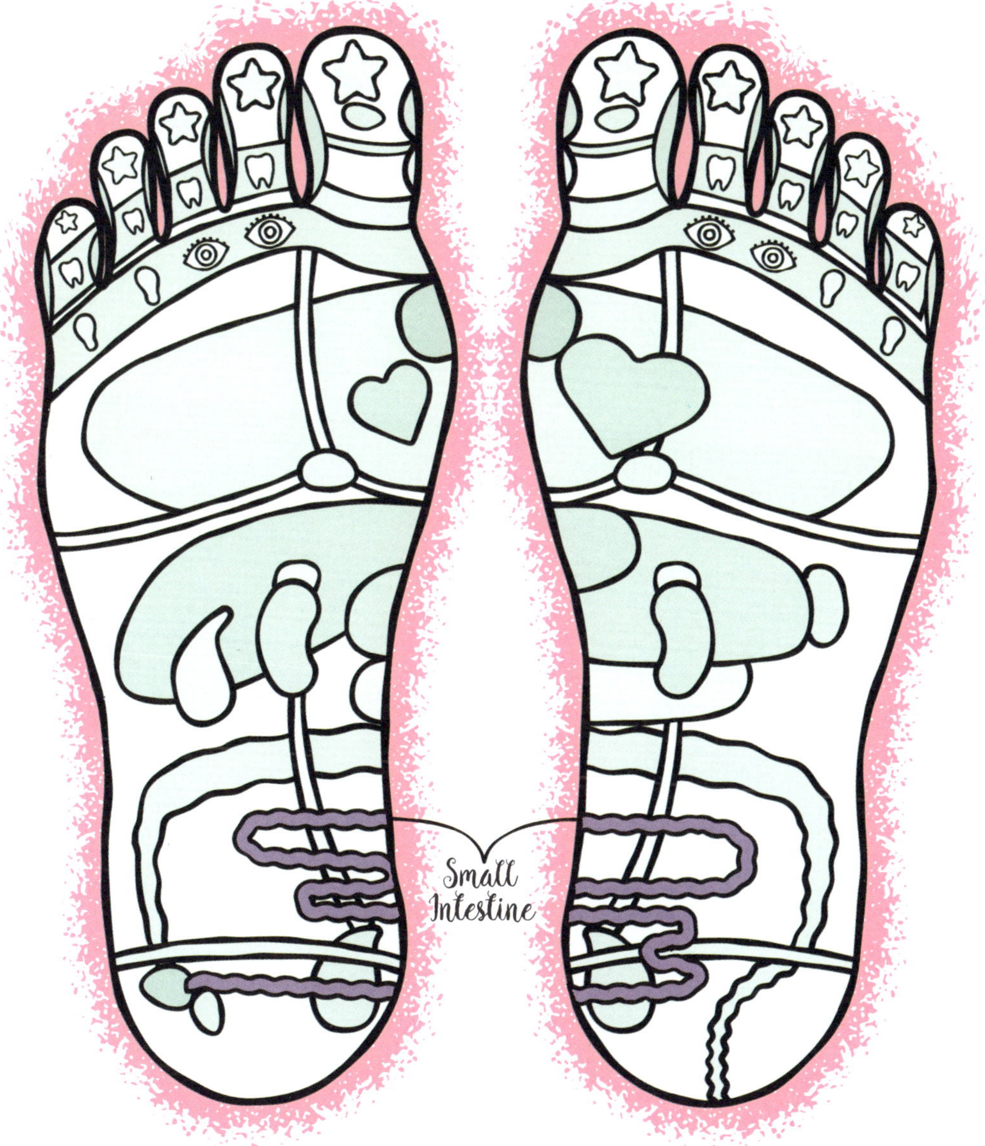

SOFT SOLE FOR UPPER AND MID ABDOMEN

COLON

The colon reflex is located in the lower part of the soft sole and heel of both feet. It begins on the right foot, close to the outer edge of the heel, and continues up to the mid soft sole. From there it continues across, from the right foot to the left foot, before descending down the soft sole, close to the outer edge, and ending on the lower heel.

How to work the reflex

For best results when working the colon reflex, it is advisable to work all of the lower soft sole and heel of both feet. The colon starts on the right side of the body, so begin with the right foot. Place the pad of your thumb at the inner edge on the mid soft sole. Use the thumb-roll technique all the way across to the outer edge of the foot. Continue working the lower soft sole, edging a little closer to the heel with each pass, until you reach the heel. Change direction at this point, working from outer edge to inner edge, until you have covered the entire heel. Repeat on the left foot, reflexing the entire lower soft sole and heel.

Work the colon reflex with a slow and rhythmical thumb roll until the tissue of the soft sole and heel softens. Hold any sensitive areas with gentle thumb pressure until the area becomes less tender.

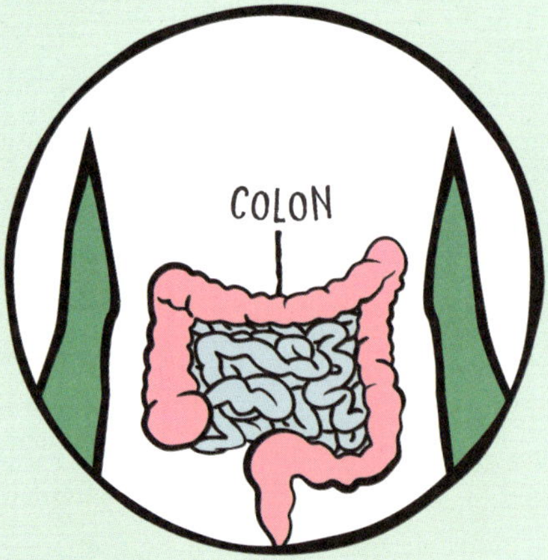

Benefits of working the reflex

The colon is the last part of the digestive system, reabsorbing fluids and processing waste products from the body. Working the colon reflex may improve digestion and help the colon to function at an optimal level.

TIP: EASE INTO IT

Revisit any particularly sensitive areas, working with light pressure until any tenderness eases.

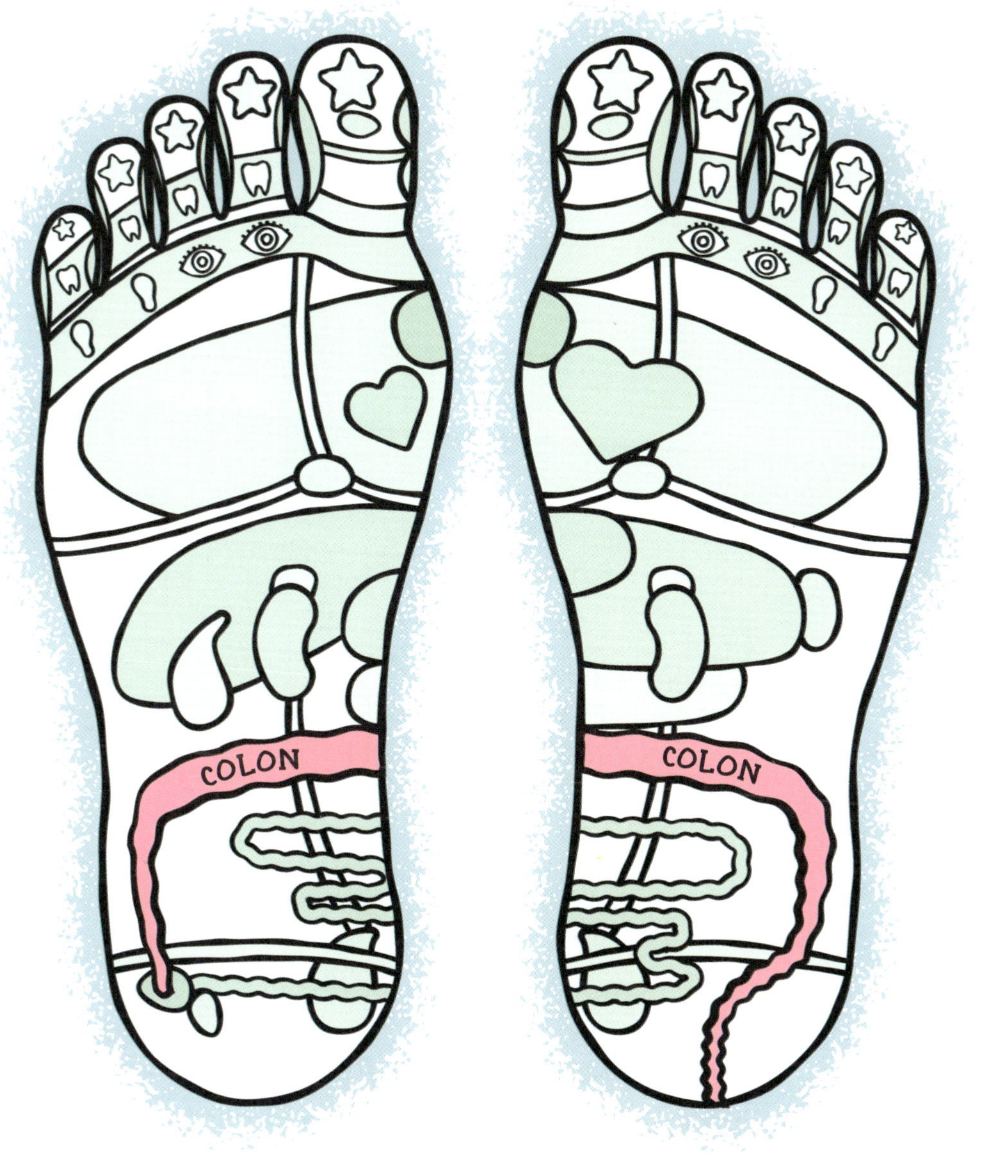

SOFT SOLE FOR UPPER AND MID ABDOMEN

SCIATIC NERVE

The sciatic nerve reflex is located on both feet between the lower soft sole and the heel.

How to work the reflex

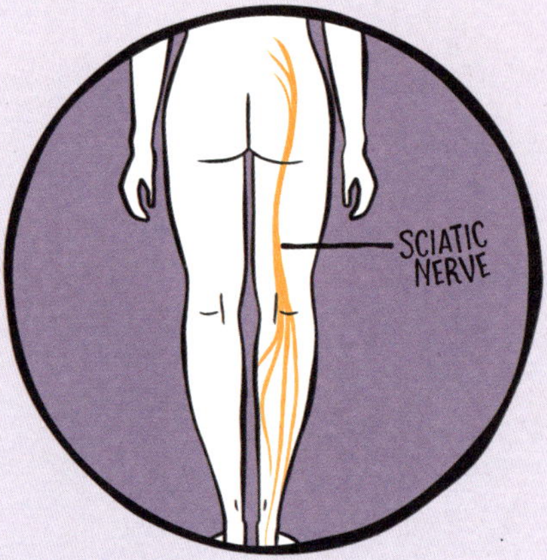

If sciatic discomfort is experienced in only one side of the body, begin working the sciatic nerve reflex of the corresponding foot. Place the pad of your thumb at the inner edge of the foot, on the lower soft sole, just above the heel. Work with your thumb-roll technique all the way across to the outer edge of the foot. Lift off your thumb and start the next pass across a little lower, working on the upper heel. Continue until you have covered the area of the lower soft sole and upper heel. Repeat the same technique in the same area on the other foot.

Benefits of working the reflex

The sciatic nerve is a large nerve that runs from the lower back down the back of each leg. Working the sciatic nerve reflex can help relax the muscles in the lower back and, over time, can provide significant relief from sciatic pain.

TIP: SLOW AND EVEN PRESSURE

Work the sciatic nerve reflex with a slow and even thumb roll until any tenderness eases.

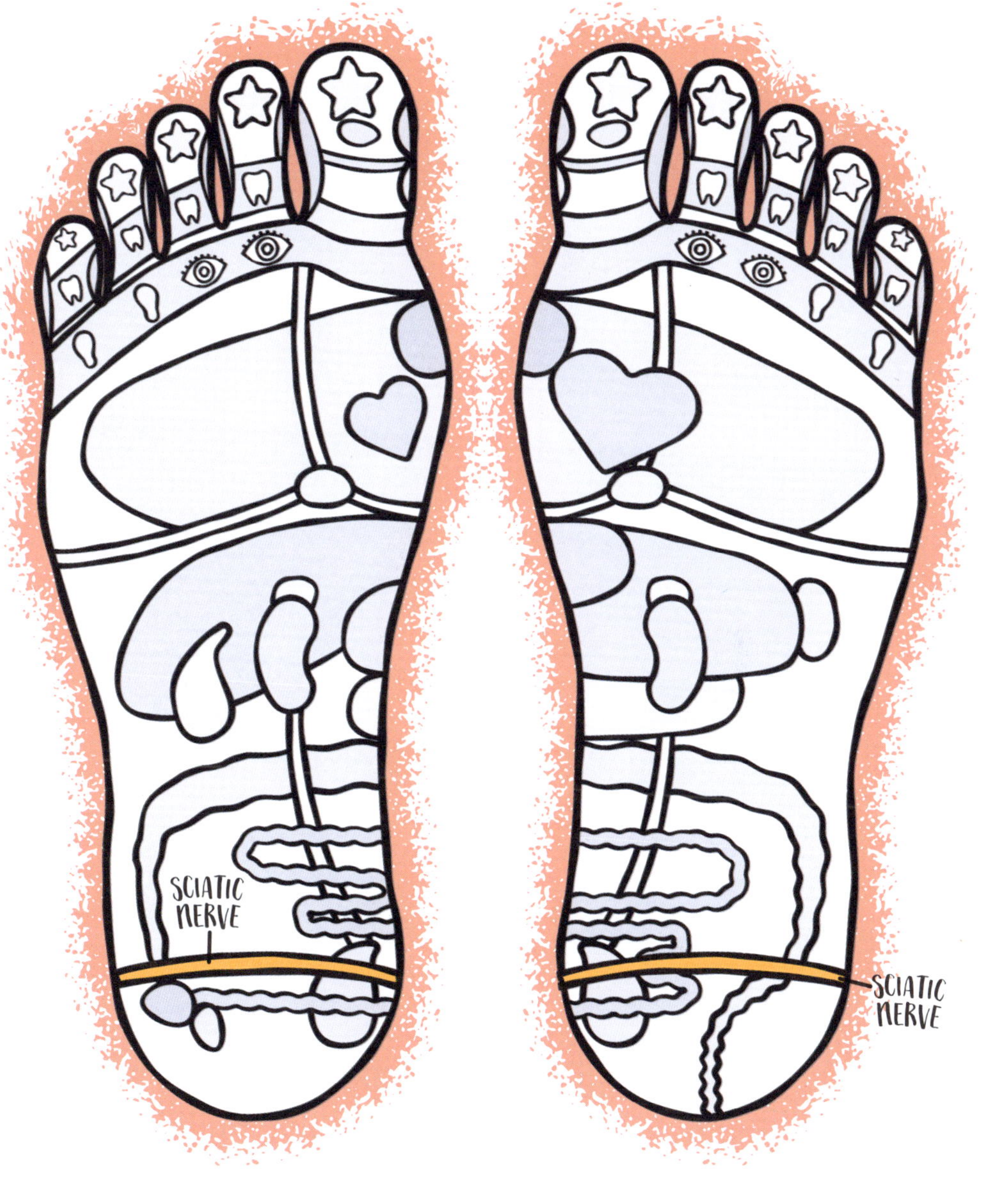

HEEL FOR LOWER ABDOMEN AND PELVIC

ILEOCECAL VALVE

The ileocecal valve reflex is located on the upper heel of the right foot, close to the outer edge.

How to work the reflex

Place the pad of your thumb on the right heel, just below the soft sole, close to the outer edge. Work with your thumb-roll technique towards the inner edge of the foot, until you have worked the area below the fifth and fourth toes. Lift off your thumb and start your thumb roll again, a little lower on the heel. Continue reflexing until you have covered most of the outer heel.

Work the ileocecal valve reflex with even thumb-roll pressure, and hold any sensitive area gently until tenderness eases off before continuing your thumb roll.

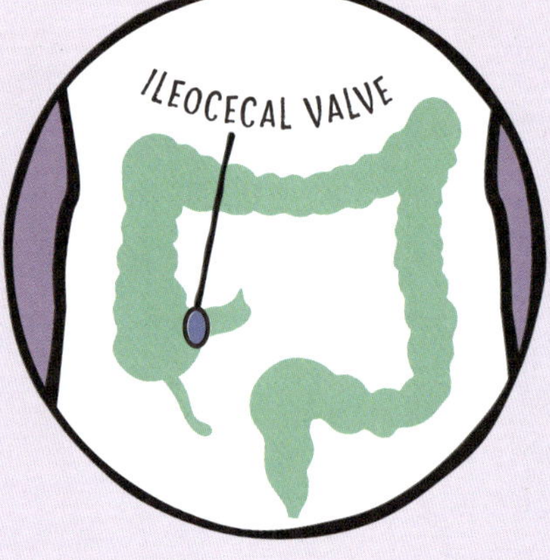

Benefits of working the reflex

As a sphincter muscle, the ileocecal valve is part of the digestive system, separating the small intestine from the colon. Working the ileocecal valve reflex can help the sphincter muscle function better and help improve digestion.

TIP: WORK THE WIDER AREA

The ileocecal valve has anatomical connections to the colon and the small intestine, so it is advisable to also work the area surrounding the reflex.

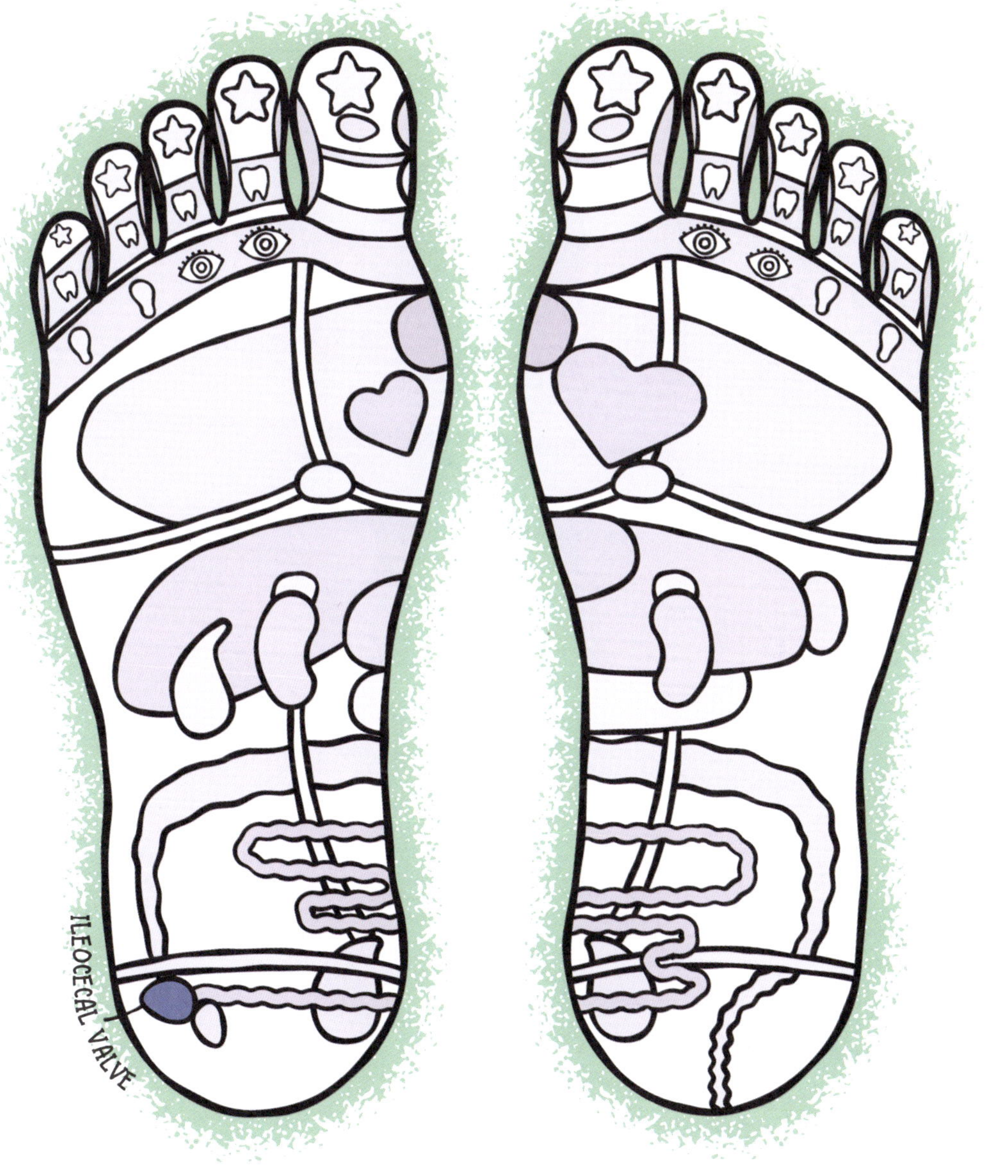

HEEL FOR LOWER ABDOMEN AND PELVIC

Appendix

The appendix reflex is located on the upper heel of the right foot, close to the outer edge.

How to work the reflex

Work the right upper heel by placing the pad of your thumb at the outer edge of the right heel, just below the soft sole. Work with your thumb-roll technique towards the inner edge, until you have reached halfway across the foot. Lift off your thumb and start your thumb roll again, this time a little lower on the heel. Continue reflexing until you have covered most of the outer half of the heel.

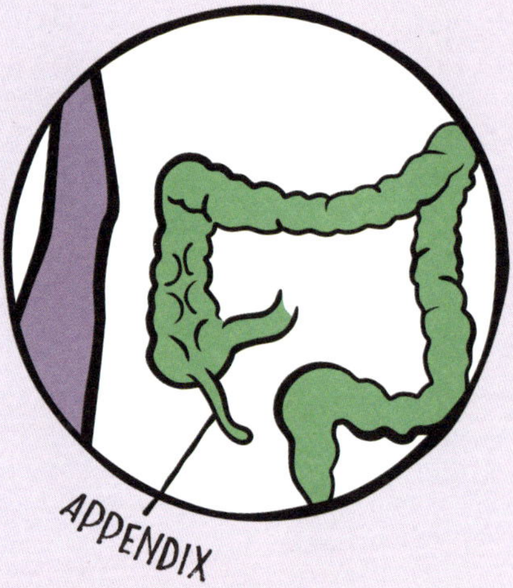

Benefits of working the reflex

The appendix plays a role in the immune system and is said to be a keeper of good gut bacteria. Working the appendix reflex can help reduce appendix pain. Seek immediate medical help if experiencing severe appendix pain – it could be appendicitis (inflammation of the appendix).

TIP: EASING TENDERNESS

Work the appendix reflex with slow and even pressure. If any area is more sensitive, keep working with lighter pressure until any tenderness eases off.

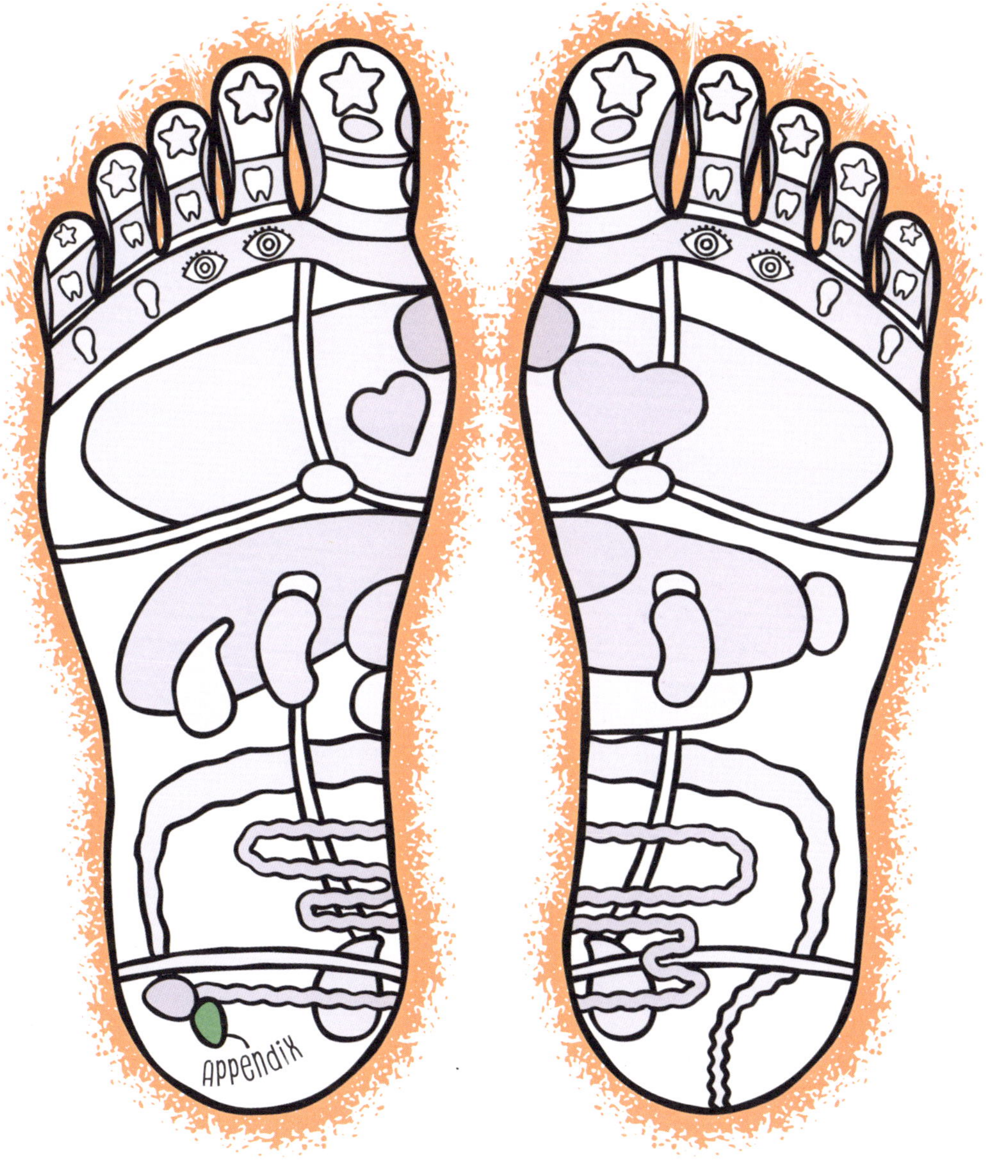

HEEL FOR LOWER ABDOMEN AND PELVIC

GROIN

The groin reflex is located on top of both feet, in the ankle groove, between the lower leg and the foot.

How to work the reflex

Before working the groin reflex, it is helpful to relax the foot so that the ankle groove is not too tight. Hold the tips of your index, middle and ring fingers of both hands next to each other and place them together in the ankle groove. Hold with firm pressure for a few seconds, and release. Repeat this technique a few times. Next, with the fingers still in the ankle groove, move the skin underneath your fingers gently to the right and then to the left, without sliding the fingers on the skin. Once the foot is relaxed, place the pad of your thumb in the ankle groove, at the inner ankle bone. Start working with your thumb-roll technique up to the centre of the groove. Repeat the same technique from the outer ankle bone to the centre of the groove.

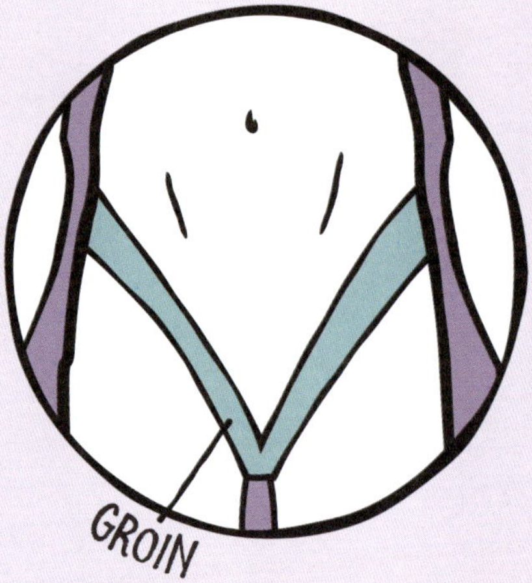

Benefits of working the reflex

Many lymph nodes can be found in the groin area, as well as the fallopian tubes (oviducts) in women and the sperm ducts in men. Working the groin reflex can help relax the groin muscles, improving circulation in the lower extremities and strengthening the immune system. It may also improve fertility.

TIP: BEWARE OF SWELLING

If the ankle groove is swollen or if there is edema, use light pressure as the groove might be quite tender.

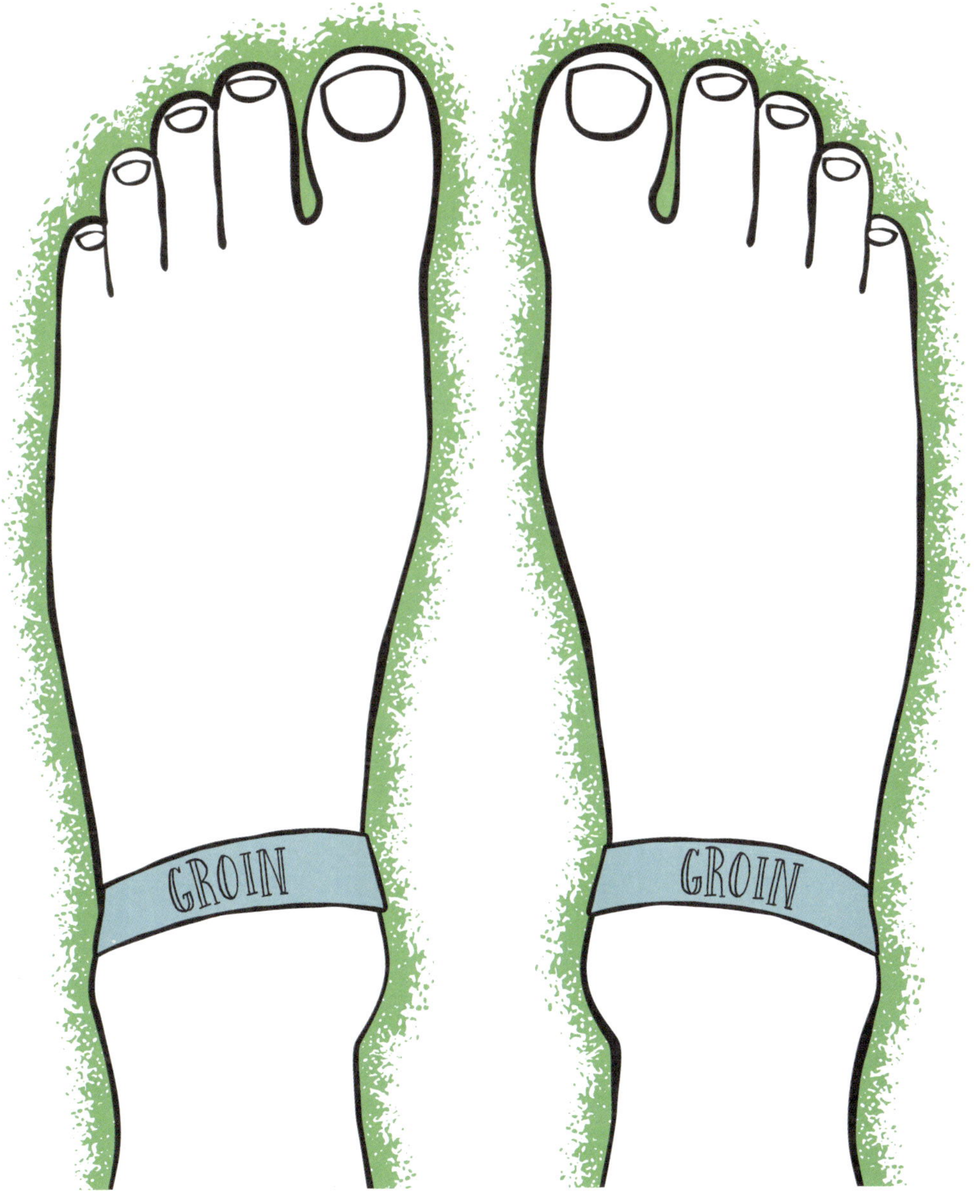

HEEL FOR LOWER ABDOMEN AND PELVIC

URINARY BLADDER

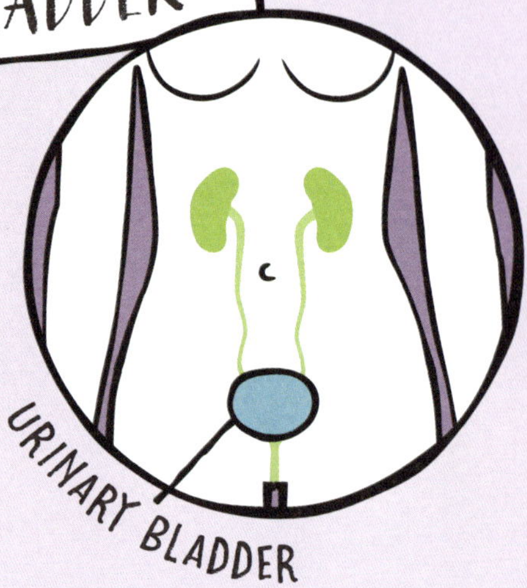

The urinary bladder reflex is located on both feet, partially on the inner edge below the ankle, and the pelvic line on the heel.

How to work the reflex

Place your thumb on the inner edge of the left foot below the ankle, just above the pelvic line. Work with your thumb roll towards the sole of the foot until you have covered the area of the inner edge and a small part of the lower soft sole. Lift off your thumb and start to work from the inner edge to the sole, this time working directly on the pelvic line. With the next pass, work the urinary bladder reflex below the pelvic line, from the inner edge to the heel. Continue working the entire urinary bladder reflex on the left foot for some time before working on the right foot in the same area with the same technique. As always, lighten the pressure or hold any sensitive areas until the tenderness eases.

Benefits of working the reflex

Working the urinary bladder reflex may assist in maintaining good bladder health.

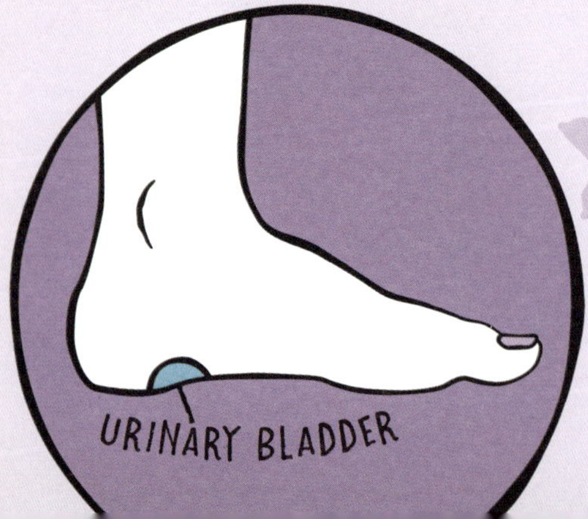

TIP: A COMON RESPONSE

When you have worked the urinary bladder reflex with an even thumb roll on both feet for a while, it is common that the receiver feels an urge to urinate.

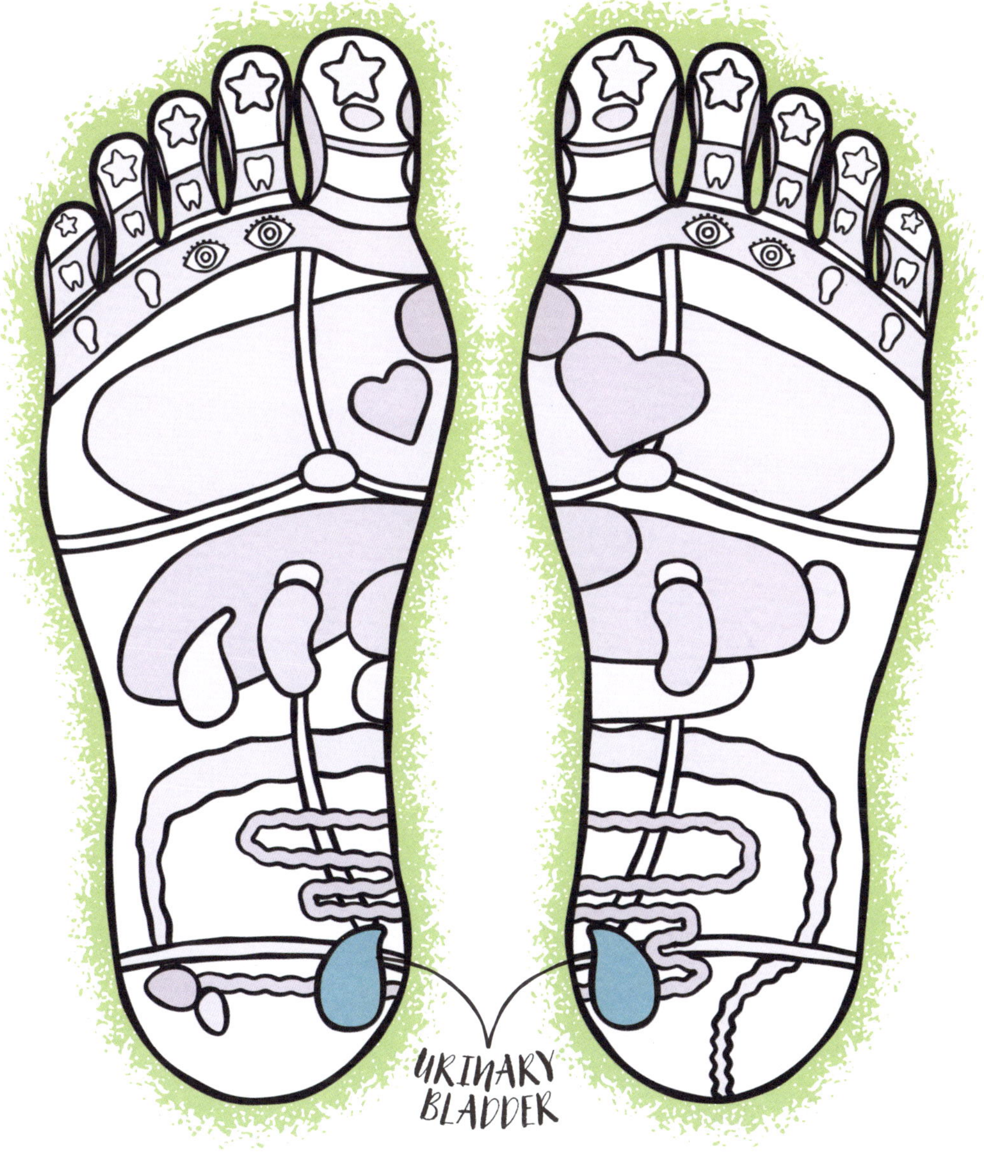

HEEL FOR LOWER ABDOMEN AND PELVIC

NECK/CERVICAL SPINE

The neck reflex is located on the inner edge of the big toe. The reflex for the neck muscles is located on the lower half of the big toe.

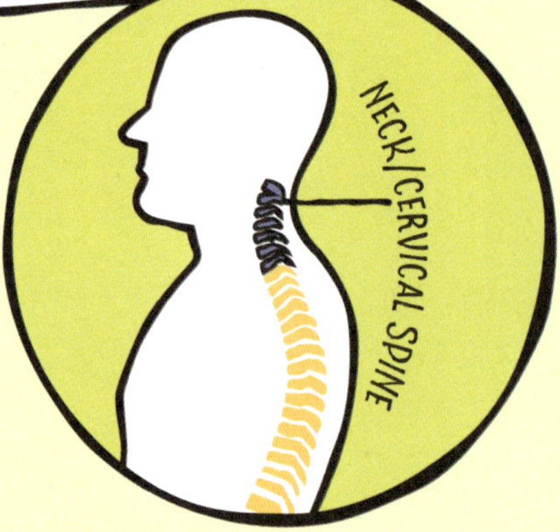

How to work the reflex

Place the pad of your thumb on the inner edge of the left big toe, close to the tip. Start your thumb-roll technique along the inner edge, towards the heel, until you have reached the base of the big toe. Repeat this technique several times. To address the neck muscles, reflex the entire base of the big toe. Place the pad of your thumb at the inner edge of the big toe, just below the joint, and work all the way across the toe. Lift off your thumb and start the next pass across a little closer to the foot. Continue reflexing horizontally until you have completed all of the lower part of the big toe. After you have finished reflexing the left foot, repeat both areas on the big toe with the same techniques on the right foot.

Benefits of working the reflex

Working the neck reflex on both feet can help relax the neck muscles, ease tension in your neck and reduce aches and pains.

TIP: WORK BOTH FEET

Always work the neck reflex on both feet, even if the discomfort is experienced only on one side of the body.

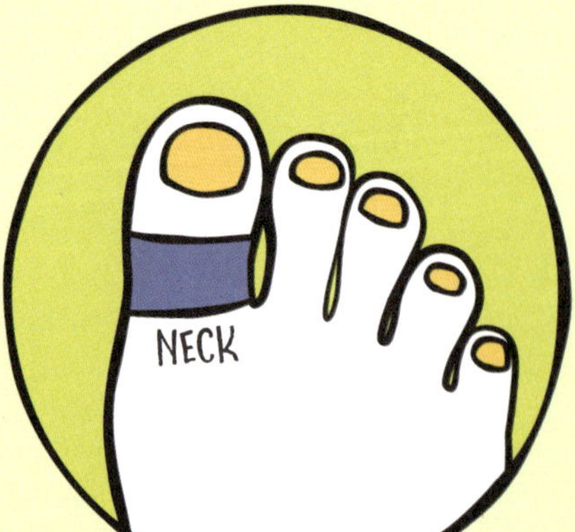

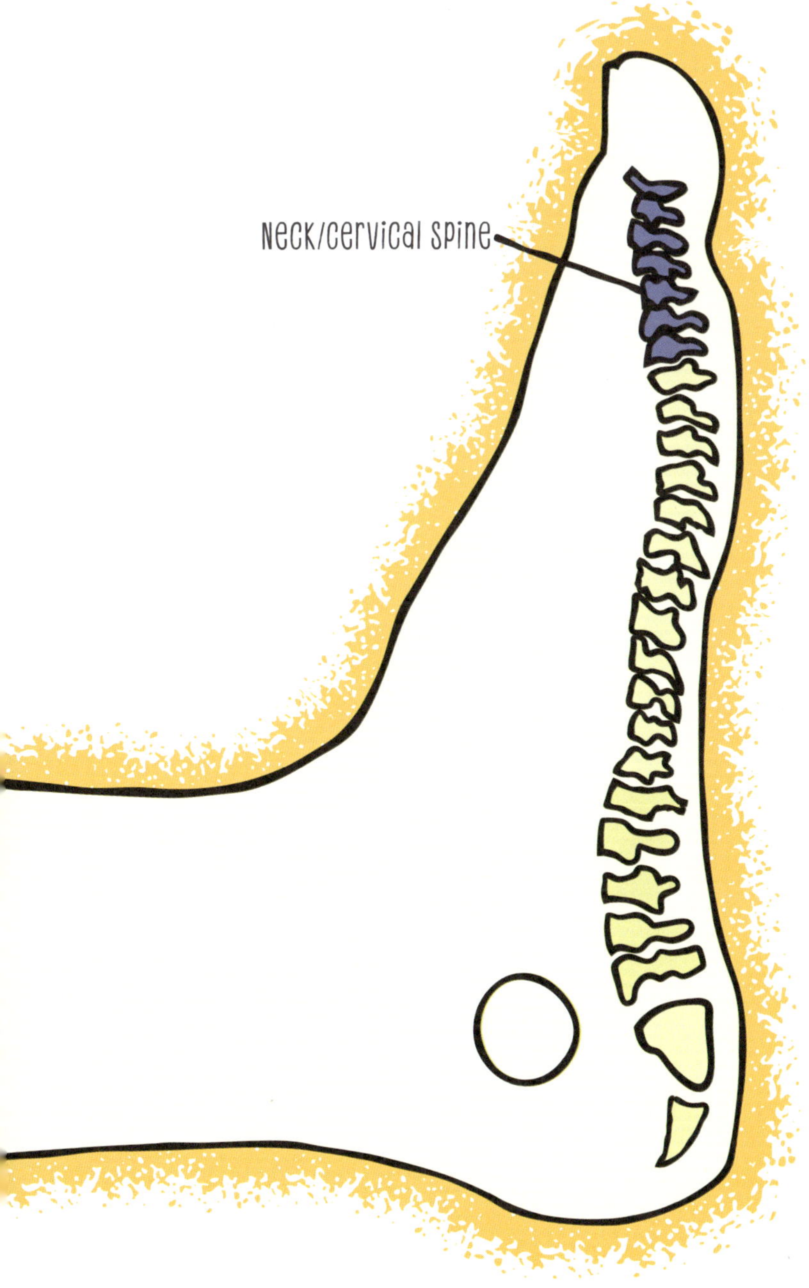

INNER EDGE FOR MIDLINE AND SPINAL

Upper back / Thoracic spine

The upper back reflex is located on the mid area of the inner edge on both feet, starting halfway between the big toe and the heel and ending at the base of the big toe.

How to work the reflex

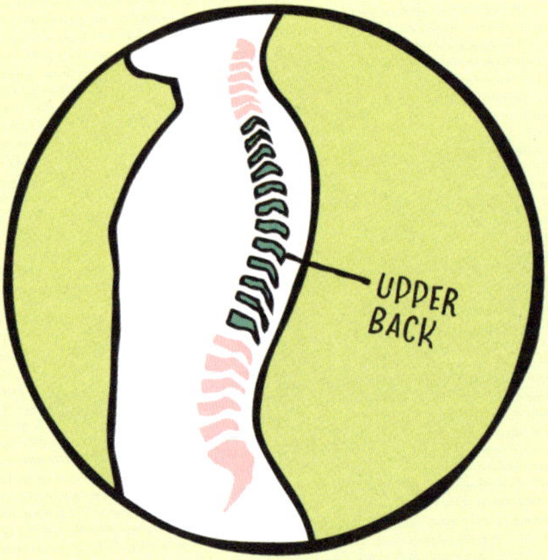

Begin reflexing the left foot by placing the pad of your thumb on the inner edge of the foot, halfway between the big toe and the heel. Start your thumb roll up towards the toes until you have reached the base of the big toe. For best results, work on the soft side next to the long bone. Repeat, reflexing upwards, several times. If the tissue underneath the skin feels harder than usual, or if it is tender to touch, stop and hold that area for a moment before continuing to reflex over it with lighter pressure. Keep reflexing until you feel the tissue soften and any tenderness eases. After you have finished working the left foot, repeat the same technique in the same area on the right foot.

Benefits of working the reflex

The thoracic spine sits in the upper section of the back. This part of the spinal column is sandwiched between the cervical spine in the neck (see pages 94–95) and the lumbar spine in the lower back (see pages 98–99). Working the upper back reflex on both feet can help relax the muscles attached to your thoracic spine. This can ease tension in your upper back, reduce aches and pains and be beneficial to other organs and glands.

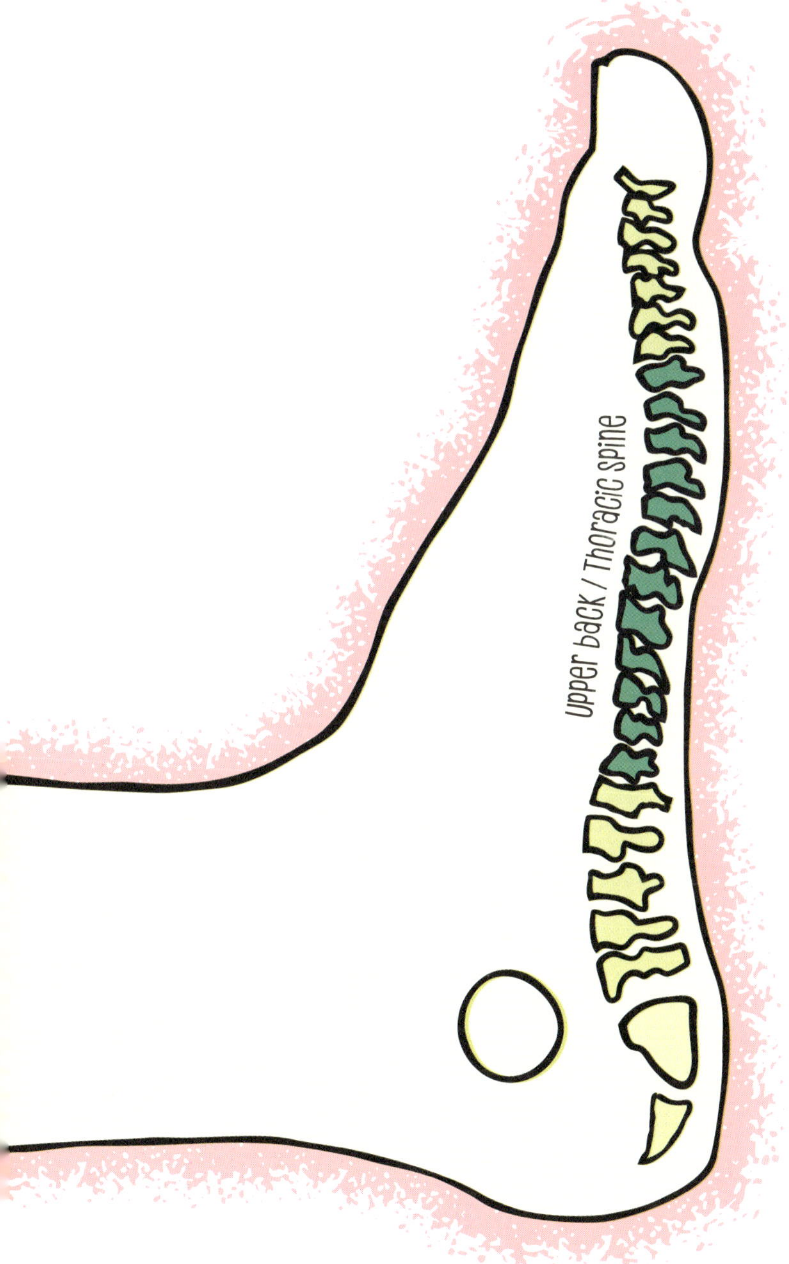

INNER EDGE FOR MIDLINE AND SPINAL

Lower Back/Lumbar Spine

You'll find the lower back reflex located on the inner edge of the arch, close to the heel.

How to work the reflex

Start your thumb-roll technique on the inner edge of your left foot, close to the heel and where the arch of your foot begins to rise. Work along the inner edge towards the toes. Lift off your thumb and start again, repeating this technique several times. If the tissue underneath the skin feels harder than usual, slightly puffy or is tender to touch, apply lighter pressure and keep reflexing until you feel the tissue soften or the area becomes less tender. After you have finished working the left foot, repeat the same technique on the right foot.

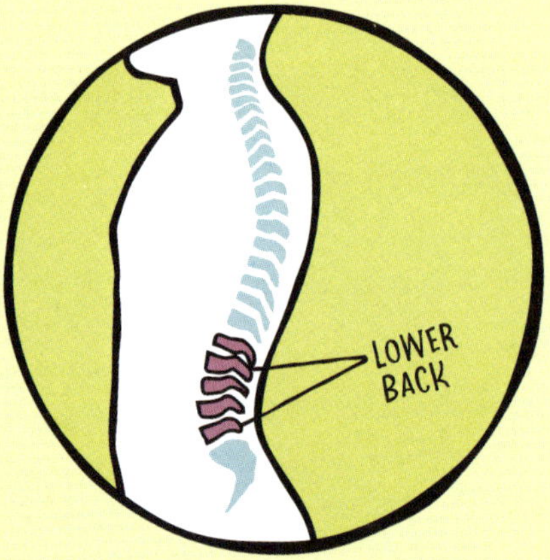

Benefits of working the reflex

The lower back reflex on your feet corresponds to the lumbar spine in your body. Working the reflex on both feet can help to relax the muscles attached to your lumbar spine. This can ease tension in your lower back, reduce aches and pains and be beneficial to other organs and glands.

TIP: AVOID VARICOSE VEINS

Don't work over varicose veins, as they are fragile and considered a contraindication.

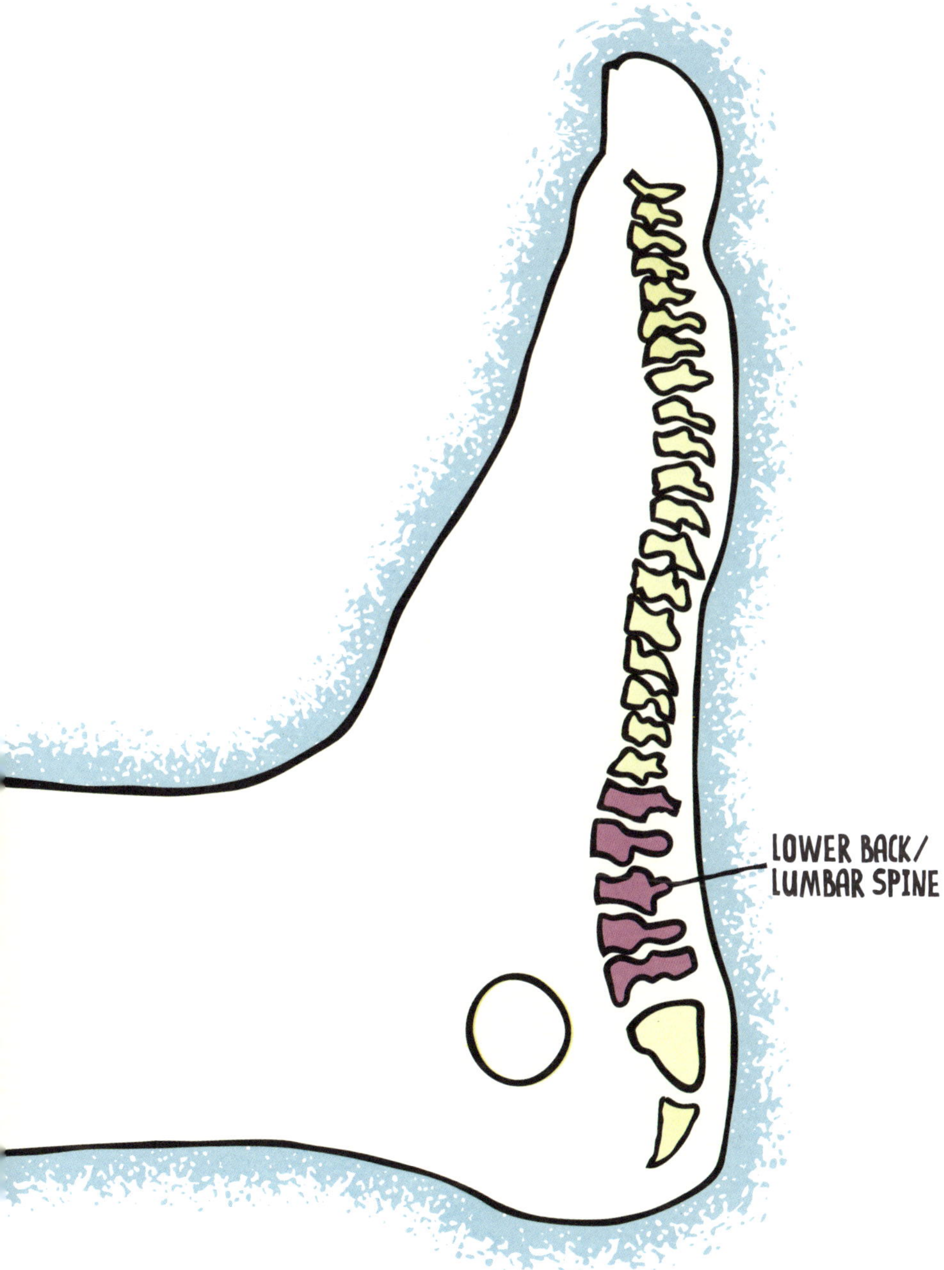

INNER EDGE FOR MIDLINE AND SPINAL

SACRUM

The sacrum reflex is located on the inner edge of both feet, below the lower back reflex (see pages 98–99) and below the ankle bone, close to the heel.

How to work the reflex

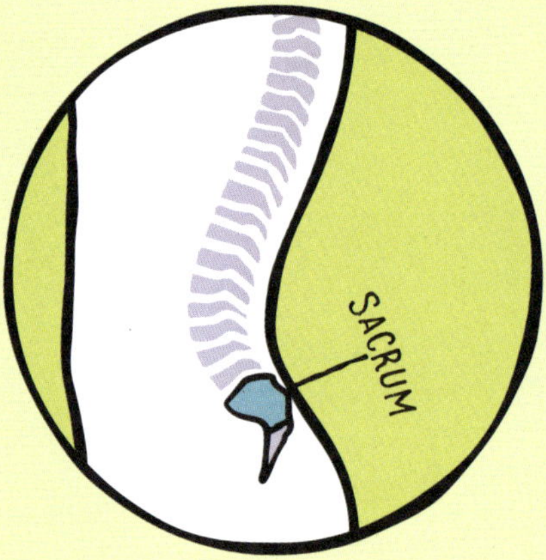

Place the pad of your thumb on the inner edge of the left foot, close to the heel, just before the arch begins to rise. Start your thumb-roll technique along the inner edge, reflexing the area below the inner ankle bone. Repeat several times. If the tissue in the sacrum reflex area feels harder than usual, slightly puffy or is tender to touch, lighten your pressure and continue reflexing over the area until you feel the tissue soften or the tenderness eases. After you have finished working the left foot, repeat the same technique in the same area on the right foot. Always work the sacrum reflex on both feet, even if the discomfort is experienced on only one side of the body.

Benefits of working the reflex

The sacrum is a triangular bone of fused vertebrae in the lower back, directly connected to the hip bones. Because the sacrum supports the weight of the upper body, many people have tension in this area. Working the sacrum reflex on both feet can help relax the muscles and ligaments attached to the sacrum. This in turn can ease tension in the entire sacrum area and reduce aches and pains.

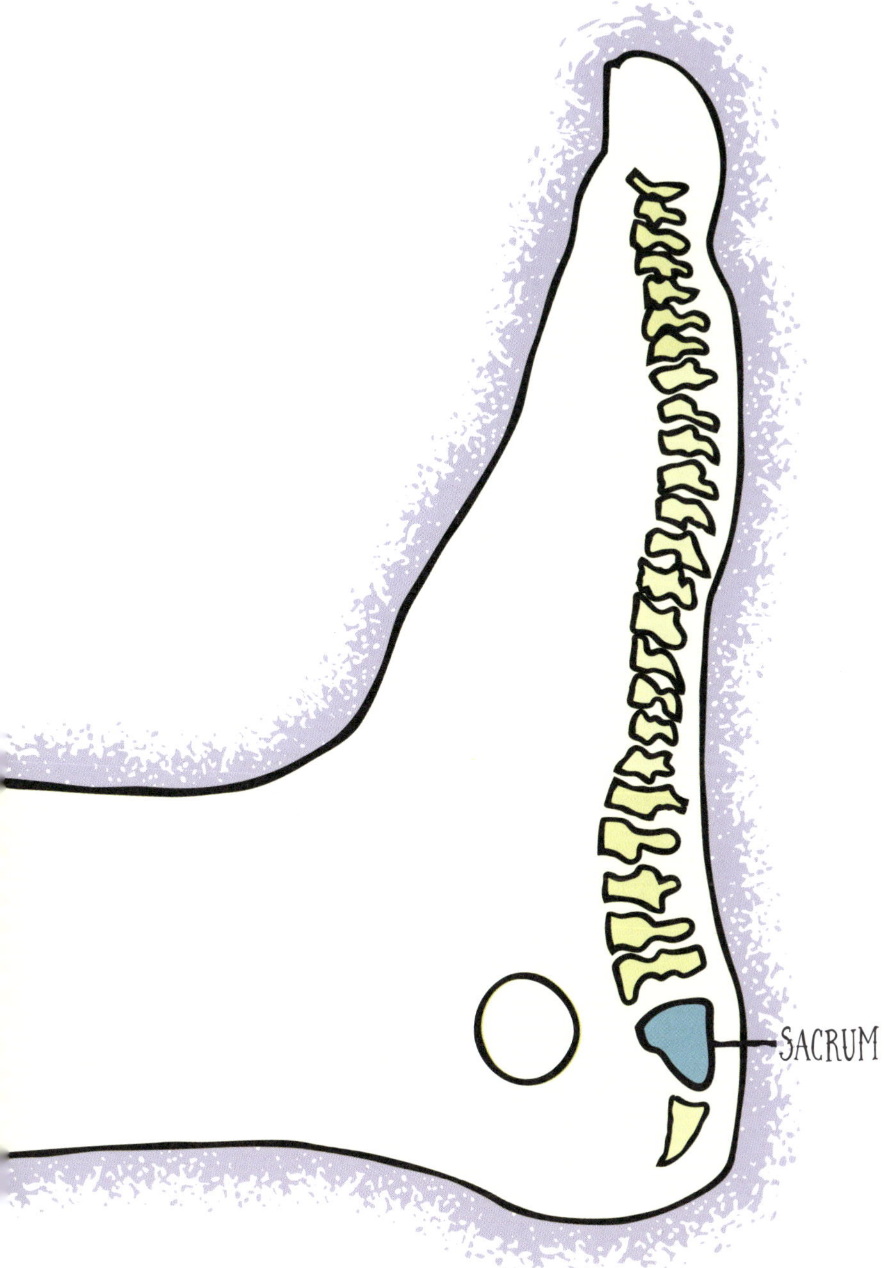

INNER EDGE FOR MIDLINE AND SPINAL

TAILBONE/COCCYX

The tailbone reflex is located on the inner edge of both feet, below the sacrum reflex (see pages 100–101), where the inner edge ends at the heel.

How to work the reflex

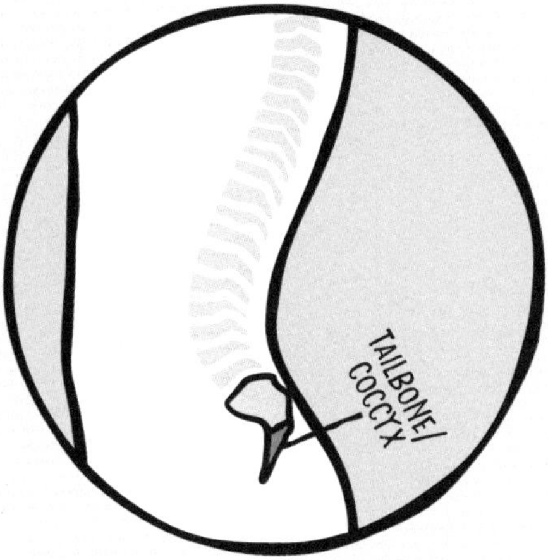

Begin by placing the pad of your thumb on the inner edge of the left foot, where it ends at the heel. Apply your thumb-roll technique to the inner edge, reflexing up towards the toes until you have covered the small area of the tailbone reflex at the bottom of the heel. Lift off your thumb and start again, continuing to work the tailbone reflex several times. If the area is tender to touch, stop and hold it for a moment before continuing to work with a lighter pressure. After you have finished the left foot, repeat the same technique in the same area on the right foot.

Benefits of working the reflex

The tailbone, or coccyx, is a small bone located at the bottom of the spine. Working the tailbone reflex on both feet can reduce aches and pains of an injured tailbone and may assist its healing process.

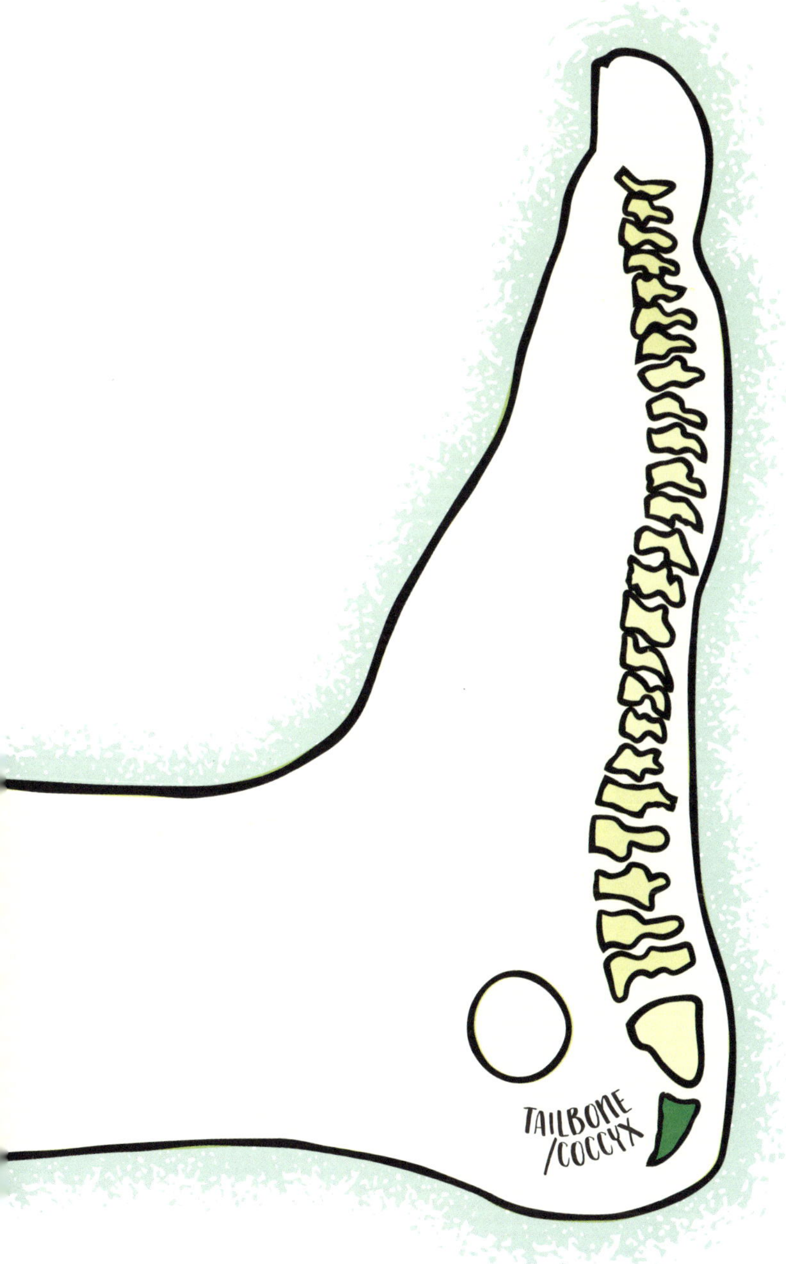

INNER EDGE FOR MIDLINE AND SPINAL

UTERUS/PROSTATE

The uterus and the prostate reflexes share the same location: they are located on the inner ankle of both feet, below and slightly behind the inner ankle bone.

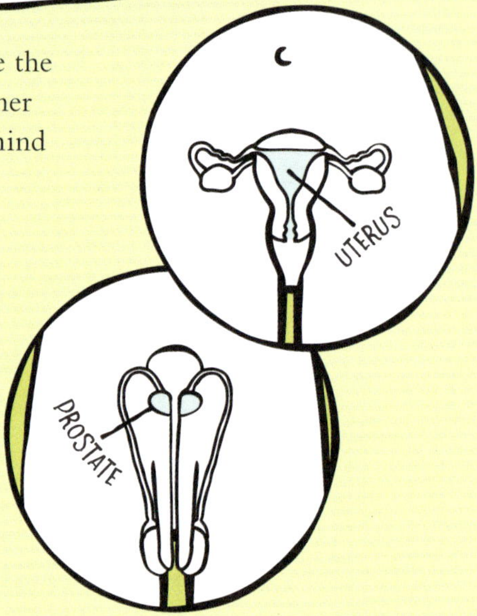

How to work the reflex

Begin by placing the pad of your thumb on the inner edge of the left foot, below the ankle bone, close to the end of the heel. Work with your thumb-roll technique along the inner edge, towards the big toe, until you have reached the area where the arch rises up. Lift off your thumb and start again, just a little closer to the ankle bone. Continue reflexing the entire inner ankle area. After you have worked the uterus/prostate reflex thoroughly, find the centre of the inner ankle and hold the area with the pad of your thumb for a minute, using firm pressure. While holding, apply slow circular movements with your thumb. After you have completed the left foot, use the same techniques on the same area on the right foot.

TIP: WORKING WITH CRAMPS

If menstrual cramps are being experienced, apply the holding technique first, until the cramps ease. When using your thumb-roll technique, work slowly, using comforting and even pressure and lightening up when you find a sensitive area.

Benefits of working the reflex

The uterus reflex on the feet corresponds to the uterus in the female body. The uterus nurtures the fertilized egg that develops into a fetus and holds a baby until birth. Working the uterus reflex can bring relief of menstrual cramps and other premenstrual symptoms (PMS). It also can help relieve symptoms of the menopause and hot flushes.

The prostate reflex on the feet corresponds to the prostate in the male body. The prostate is a small gland of the male reproductive system, situated below the urinary bladder. Working the prostate reflex may improve prostate function and assist with issues such as an enlarged prostate.

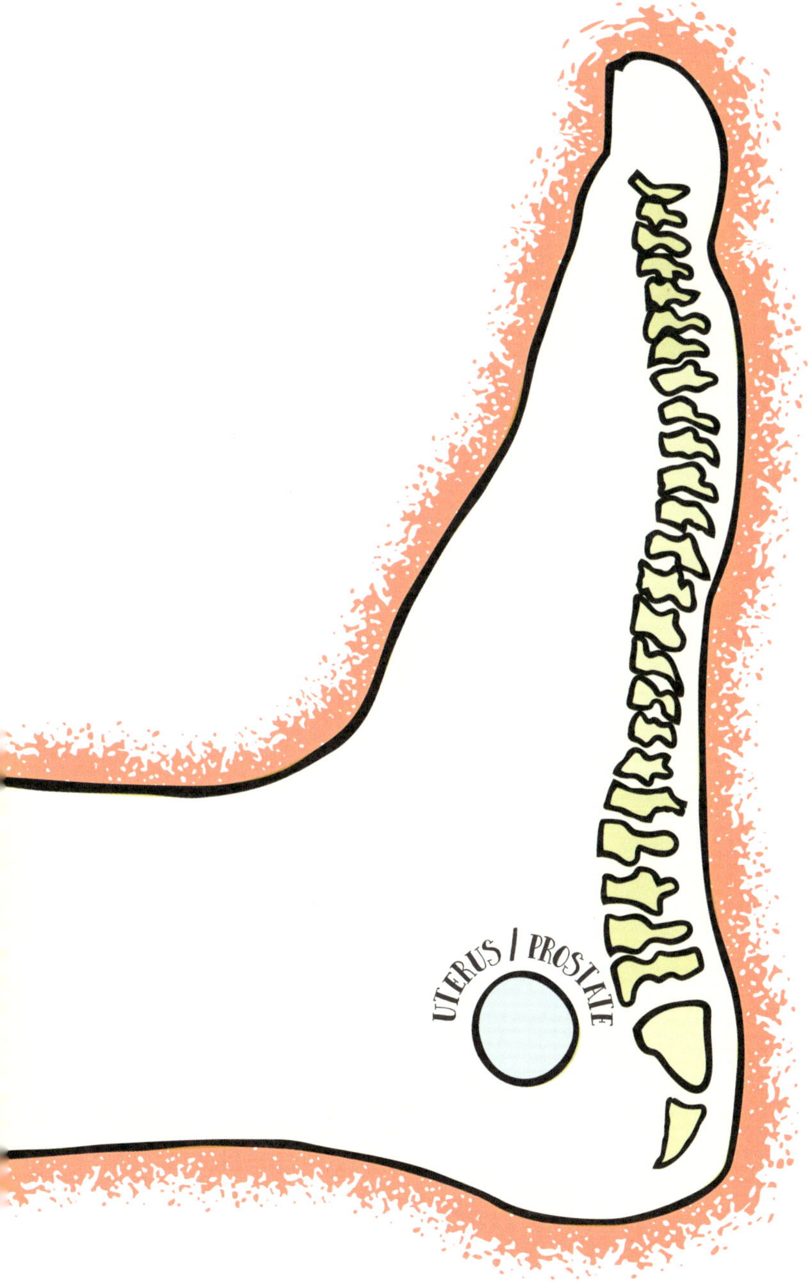

INNER EDGE FOR MIDLINE AND SPINAL

SHOULDER JOINT

The shoulder joint reflex is located on both feet, on and surrounding the joint below the little toe.

How to work the reflex

If discomfort is experienced in only one shoulder joint, begin by working the shoulder joint reflex of the corresponding foot. Place the pad of your thumb at the outer edge of the foot, directly below the little toe. Apply your thumb roll to work towards the inner edge, until you have reached the fourth toe. Lift off your thumb and start again, a little lower than before. Continue working the upper part of the pad, below the little toe. Next, place your thumb on the outer edge of the foot, about a finger-width below the little toe, and thumb-roll up until you have reached the little toe. Repeat several times. To complete the work on the shoulder joint reflex, apply a two-finger roll on top of the foot. Place the tips of your index and middle fingers next to each other, and start your finger roll directly below the little toe. With gentle pressure, work down towards the leg until you have covered the distance of a finger-width. After you have completed one foot, apply the same techniques to the shoulder joint reflex of the other foot.

Work the shoulder joint reflex on all three sides below the little toe until tenderness, if any, eases off.

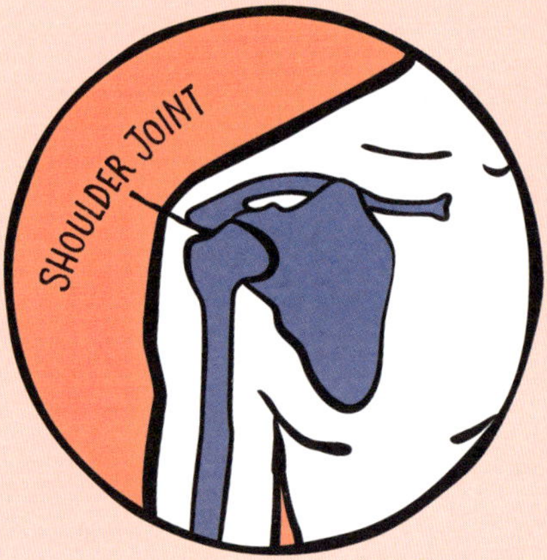

Benefits of working the reflex

The shoulder joint is the most flexible joint in the human body, held together by extensive ligaments and muscles. Working the shoulder joint reflex can help relax the shoulder muscles, reducing pain and discomfort from any form of shoulder joint issue.

TIP: BEWARE OF SENSITIVITY

The top of the foot, below the toes, may be sensitive for anatomical reasons.

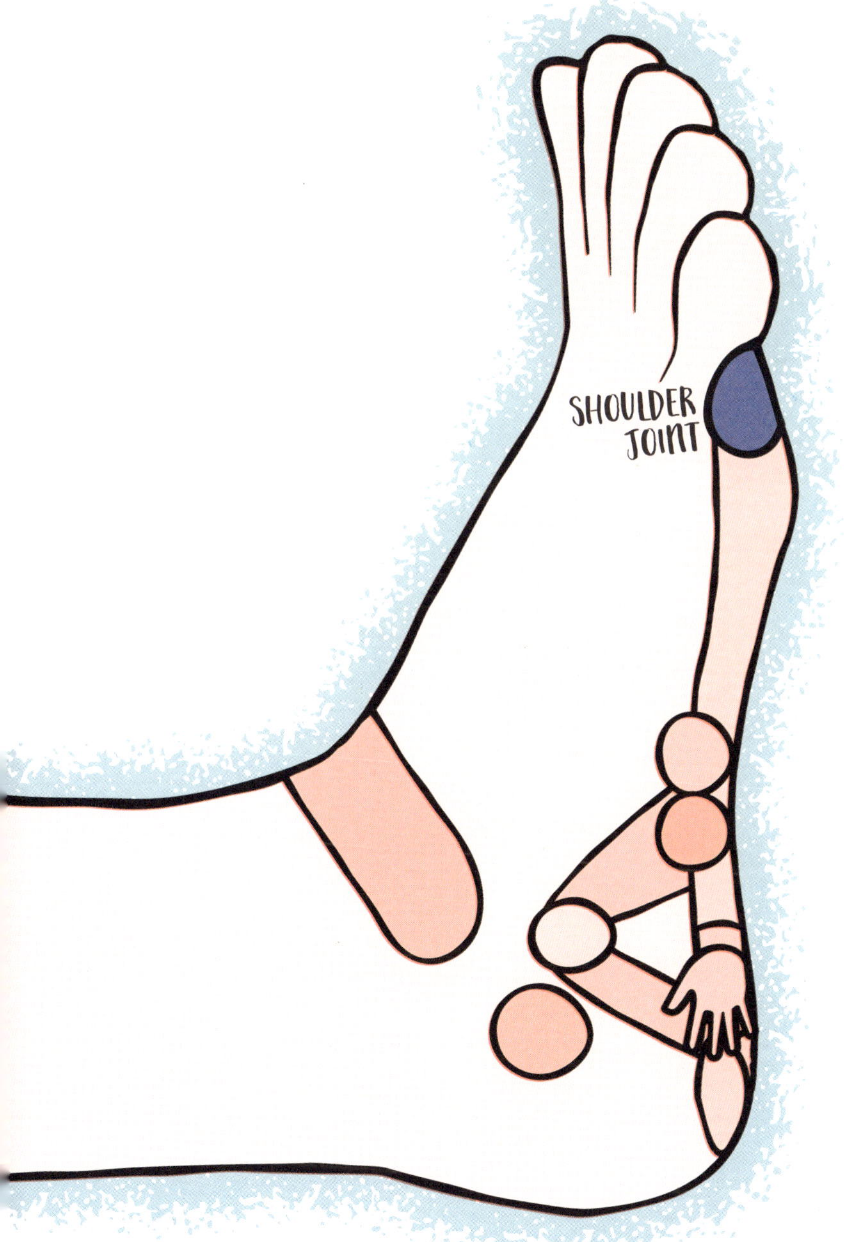

OUTER EDGE FOR ARMS AND LEGS

ARMS

The arm reflex is located on the outer edge of both feet, starting with the upper arm reflex, directly below the little toe, and ending with the wrist reflex (see pages 112–113), close to the end of the outer heel.

How to work the reflex

If discomfort is being experienced in one arm, begin working the arm reflex of the corresponding foot. Place the pad of your thumb on the outer edge of the foot, close to the end of the heel. Work with your thumb-roll technique up towards the toes until you have reached the base of the little toe. Lift off your thumb and repeat, working the entire length of the arm reflex several times. If you are experiencing discomfort in the upper arm, emphasize working the upper half of the outer edge, closer to the toes. If you are experiencing discomfort in the forearm, emphasize working the lower half of the outer edge, closer to the heel. Continue reflexing over any sensitive areas with lighter thumb-roll pressure, until the tenderness eases off.

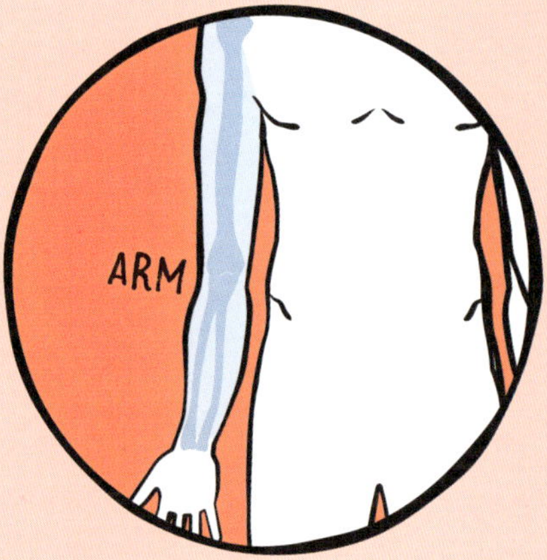

Benefits of working the reflex

Arm pain can be the result of a variety of issues. Working the arm reflex can help relax the arm muscles, ease tension and reduce general aches and pains.

TIP: WORK BOTH ARMS

If discomfort is experienced in both arms, repeat the same technique in the same area on the other foot.

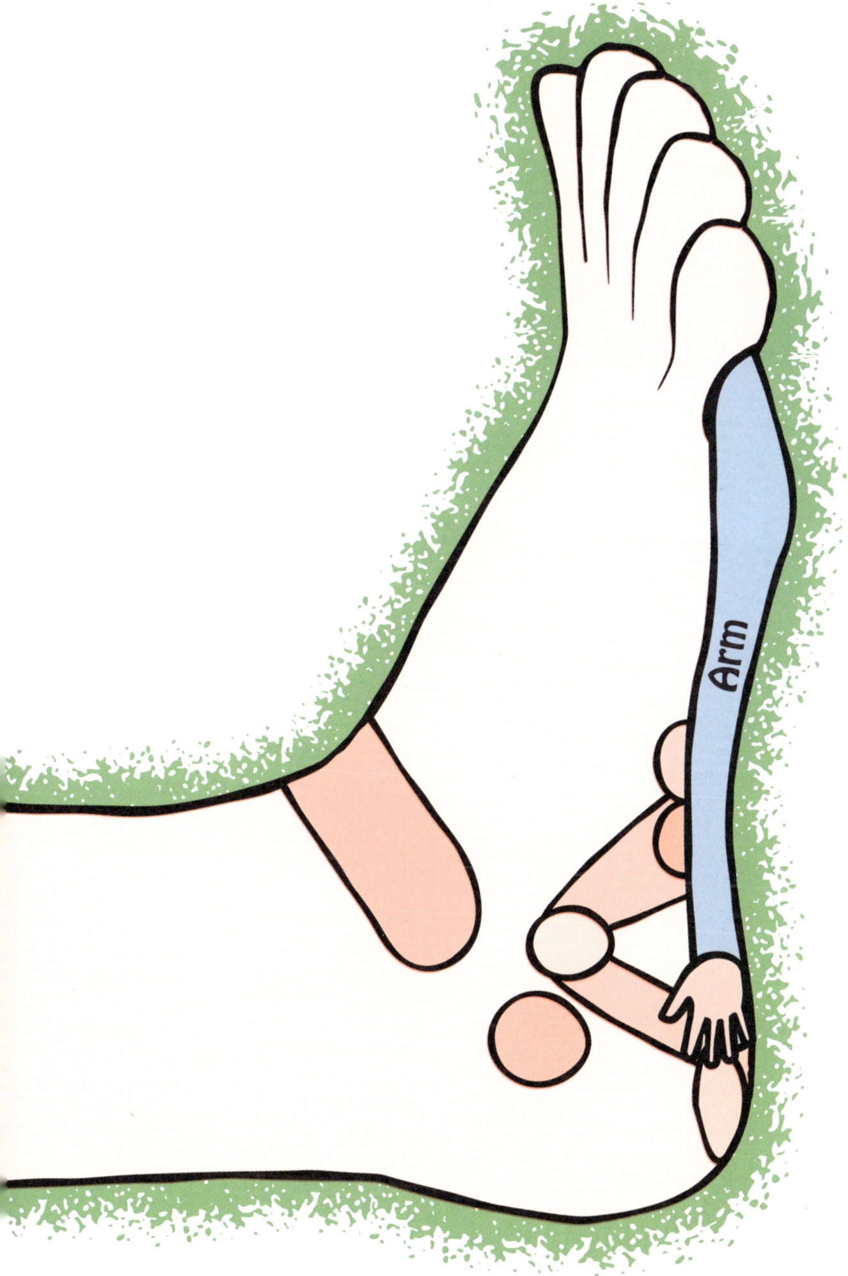

OUTER EDGE FOR ARMS AND LEGS

ELBOW

The elbow reflex is located just above the hip reflex (see pages 114–115), on the outer edge of both feet, on the bony prominence halfway between the heel and the little toe.

How to work the reflex

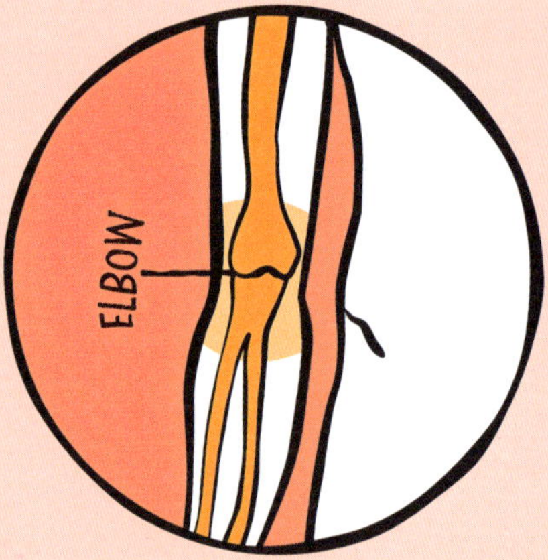

If discomfort is being experienced in one elbow, begin working the elbow reflex of the corresponding foot. Place the pad of your thumb on the outer edge of the foot, about halfway between the heel and the little toe, just below the bony prominence. Using your thumb roll, work over the bony prominence towards the little toe. Lift off your thumb and repeat several times. For extra emphasis, you can also reflex the area next to the bony prominence on the bottom of the foot, using the same thumb-roll technique. Continue reflexing the area on and around the bony prominence on the outer edge, until any tenderness eases off.

Benefits of working the reflex

Working the elbow reflex can help ease aches and pains from issues such as tennis elbow, bursitis and more.

TIP: WORKING BOTH ELBOWS

If you are experiencing discomfort in both elbows, repeat the same technique in the same area on the other foot.

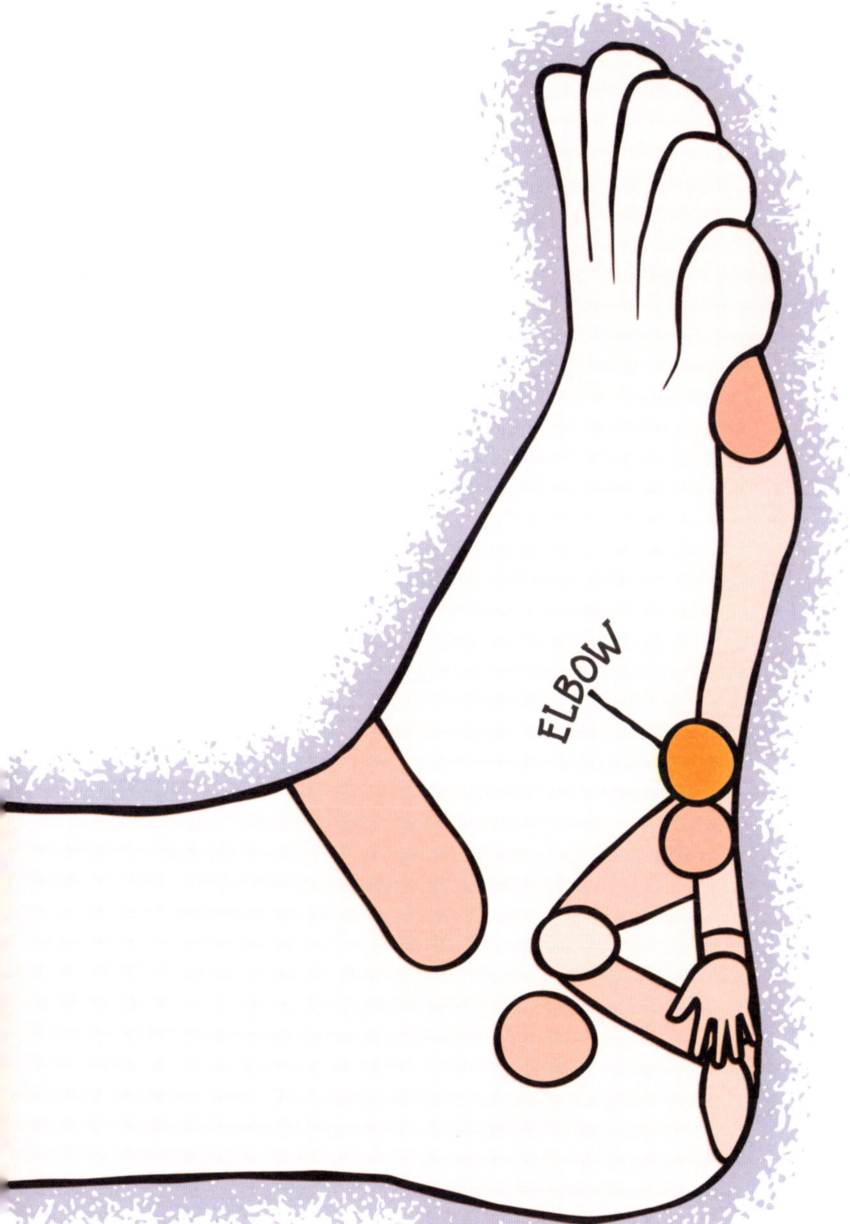

OUTER EDGE FOR ARMS AND LEGS

HANDS/WRISTS

The hand and wrist reflex is located on the outer edge of both feet, close to the heel.

How to work the reflex

If discomfort is being experienced in one hand or wrist, begin working the hand and wrist reflex of the corresponding foot. Place the pad of your thumb on the outer edge of the foot, at the end of the heel. Work with your thumb roll up towards the little toe until you have covered half of the heel's length. Lift off your thumb and start again, this time a little closer to the ankle bone. Continue working most of the lower heel on the outer edge of the foot.

If you are experiencing discomfort in both hands or wrists, repeat the same technique in the same area on the other foot.

Benefits of working the reflex

We all know that the wrist connects the hand to the forearm, but we don't always know the issues causing hand and wrist pain. Working the hand and wrist reflex can help ease aches and pains and may relieve discomfort associated with carpal tunnel syndrome.

TIP: WORK THE WIDER AREA

Because every person is different and the hand and wrist reflex is a small area, it is recommended to work the broader area on the outer heel, as described above, to make sure that all of the hand and wrist reflex is covered.

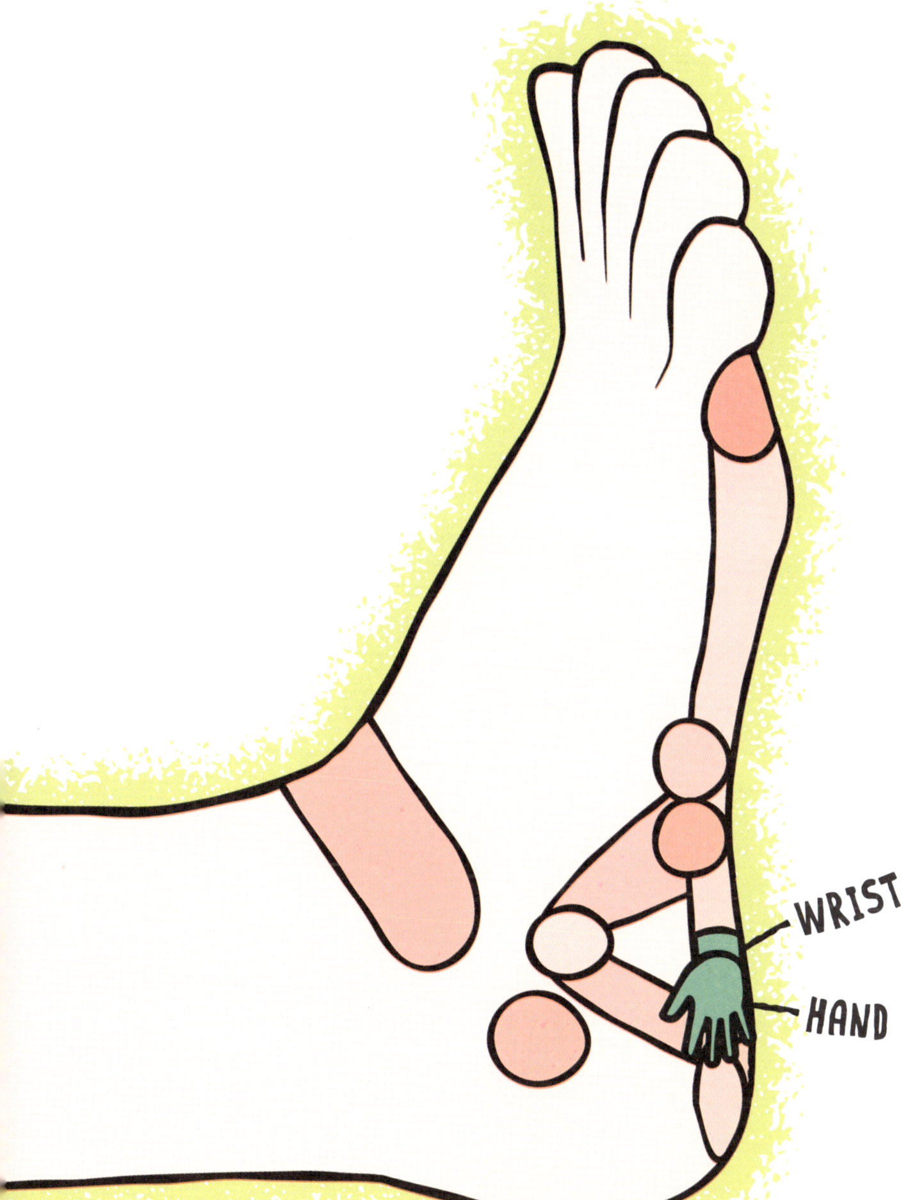

OUTER EDGE FOR ARMS AND LEGS

HIP

The hip reflex is located on the outer edge of both feet, just below the elbow reflex (see pages 110–111) and the bony prominence, close to the heel.

How to work the reflex

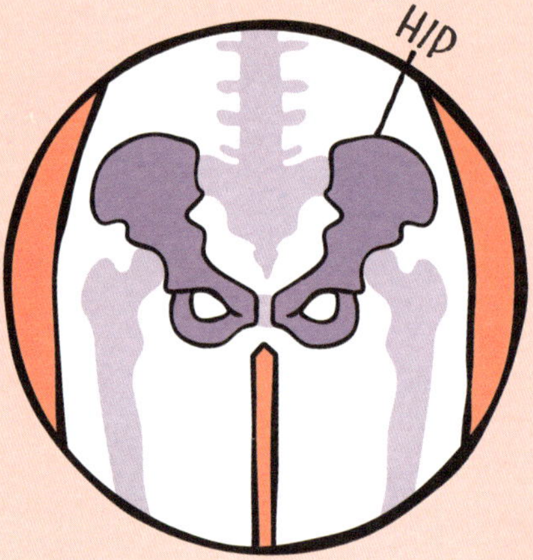

If discomfort is experienced in one hip, work the hip reflex of the corresponding foot first. Place the pad of your thumb on the outer edge of the foot, below the ankle bone. Work with your thumb roll up towards the little toe, until you have reached the bony prominence. Repeat, working the hip reflex several times with a slow and even thumb roll. If there is any tenderness, stop and hold that area for a moment before continuing to reflex over it with lighter pressure. Keep reflexing until you feel the tissue soften and any tenderness eases off. After you have finished working one foot, repeat the same technique in the same area on the other foot.

Benefits of working the reflex

The hips are two of the most important joints in our body, allowing us to walk, run and jump. Working the hip reflex can help relax muscles attached to the hip, relieve aches and pains and may assist in the healing process after hip injury and hip replacement.

TIP: BALANCE THE HIPS

A strained hip on one side of the body has a direct influence on the other hip. Always work the hip reflex on both feet, even if discomfort is experienced in only one side of the body.

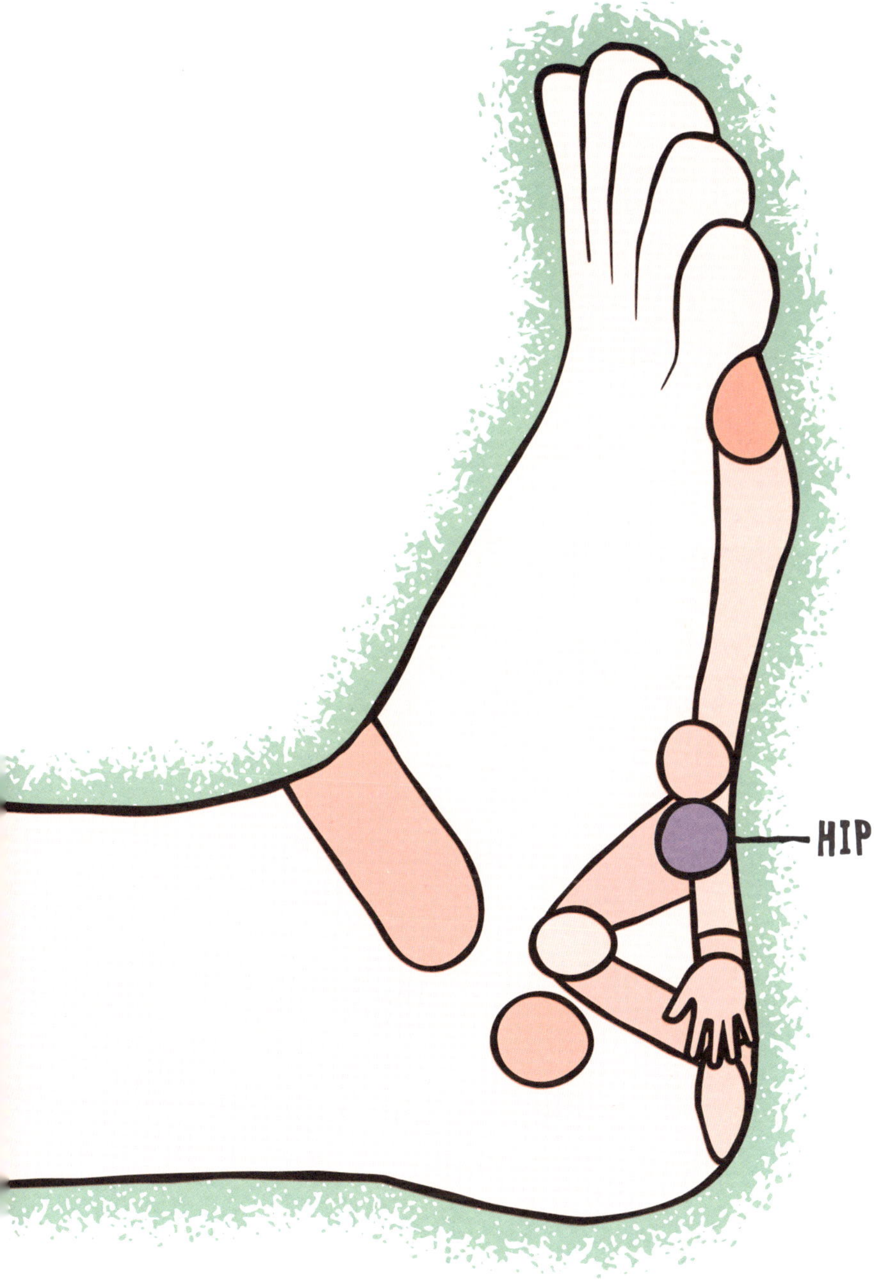

OUTER EDGE FOR ARMS AND LEGS

Legs

The leg reflex is located on both feet, on the lower half of the outer edge, in the soft-tissue triangle below and slightly in front of the ankle bone.

How to work the reflex

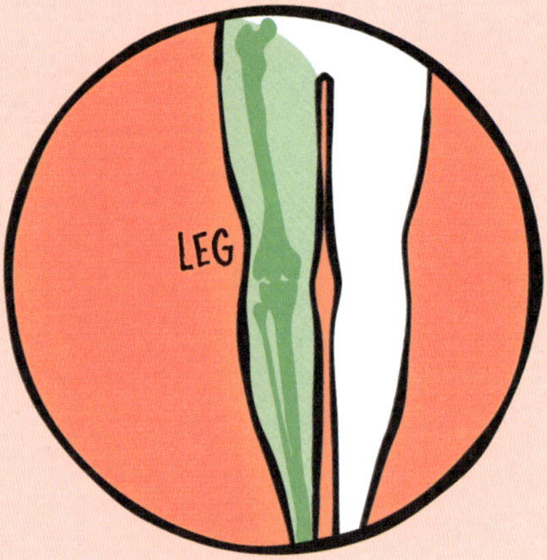

If the discomfort is being experienced in only one leg, begin working the leg reflex of the corresponding foot. Place the pad of your thumb on the outer edge of the foot, at the end of the heel. Work with your thumb roll up towards the little toe until you have reached the bony prominence, halfway up the outer edge. Lift off your thumb and start again at the heel, a little closer to the ankle bone. Continue reflexing the entire outer heel and the soft-tissue triangle below the ankle bone several times. If the tissue in the area below the ankle bone feels harder than usual or if the area is sensitive, continue reflexing over it with lighter pressure until the tissue softens or tenderness eases.

Benefits of working the reflex

Working the leg reflex can help leg muscles to relax, ease aches and pains, increase circulation in the lower limbs and help relieve leg cramps.

TIP: BALANCE THE LEGS

Discomfort in one leg often causes overuse of the other leg. For this reason, it is advisable to always work the leg reflex on both feet, even if the discomfort is experienced in only one side of the body.

OUTER EDGE FOR ARMS AND LEGS

Knees

The knee reflex is located on the outer edge of both feet, on the upper tip of the soft-tissue triangle, below and slightly in front of the ankle bone.

How to work the reflex

If discomfort is experienced in one knee, work the knee reflex of the corresponding foot first. Place the pad of your thumb on the outer edge of the foot, below and slightly in front of the ankle bone, on the upper tip of the soft-tissue triangle. Hold the area for a moment before applying gentle circular movements with your thumb, without leaving the knee reflex. You can alternate holding and circular movements for a few minutes. Next, apply your thumb roll and work the small area of the knee reflex with a few rolls towards the little toe. Repeat, working the knee reflex several times with a slow and even thumb roll.

If there is any tenderness, stop and hold that area again for a moment before continuing to reflex over it with lighter pressure. Keep reflexing until any tenderness eases. After you have finished working one foot, repeat the same techniques in the same area on the other foot.

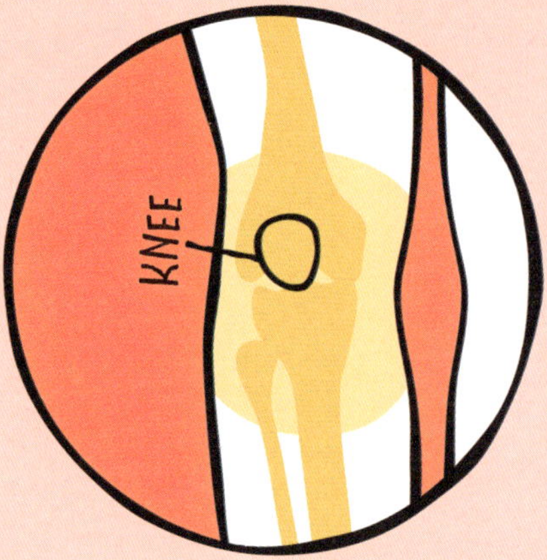

TIP: BALANCE THE KNEES

Discomfort in one knee often causes overuse of the other knee. For this reason, it is advisable to always work the knee reflex on both feet, even if the discomfort is experienced in only one side of the body.

Benefits of working the reflex

The knee joint is one of the strongest – and most used – joints in our body, supporting the body's weight, with tendons connecting the knee to the leg and ligaments providing stability. Working the knee reflex can relieve knee pain and discomfort from knee injury and other issues. It can also assist in the healing process following knee replacement.

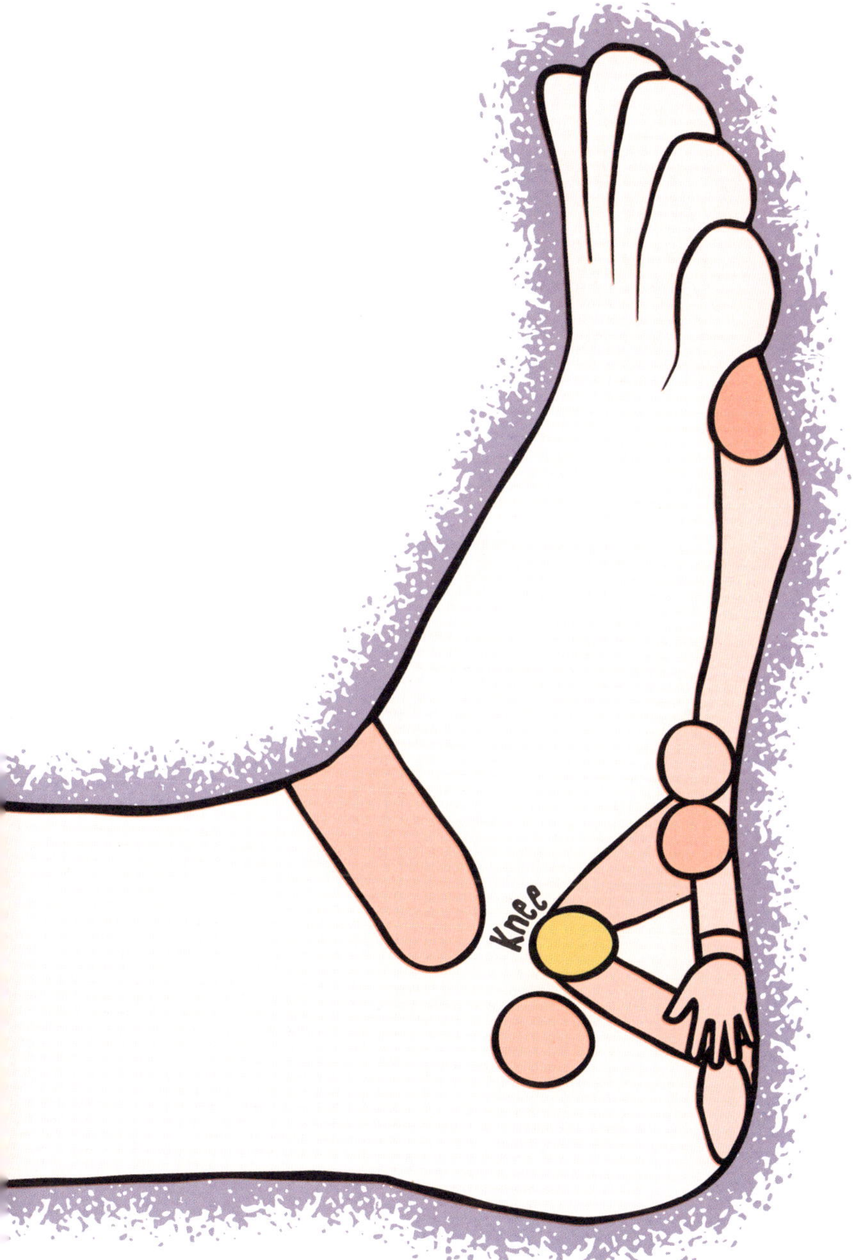

OUTER EDGE FOR ARMS AND LEGS

FOOT

The foot reflex is located on the outer edge of both feet, at the end of the heel.

How to work the reflex

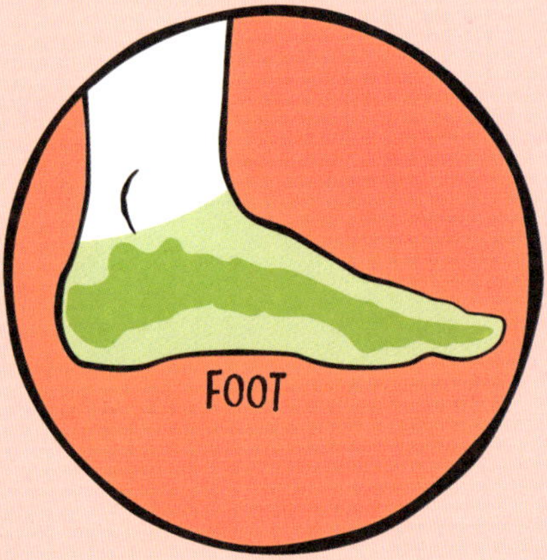

If discomfort is being experienced in one foot, begin by working that foot. Place the pad of your thumb on the outer edge of the foot at the end of the heel. Start working with your thumb roll up towards the little toe for just a few rolls. Lift off your thumb and start again at the end of the heel, just a little closer to the ankle bone. Continue reflexing over the small area of the foot reflex on the outer edge several times. Hold any sensitive area with the pad of your thumb until any tenderness eases off, before continuing to reflex with lighter pressure.

If you are experiencing discomfort in both feet, repeat the same technique in the same area on the other foot.

Benefits of working the reflex

Foot and ankle pain may be alleviated by working the foot reflex, which may also assist in the self-healing process following a foot injury.

TIP: WORK THE WIDER AREA

Every person is different, and the foot reflex is a small area, so it is advisable to work the broader area, as described above, to make sure that all of the foot reflex is covered.

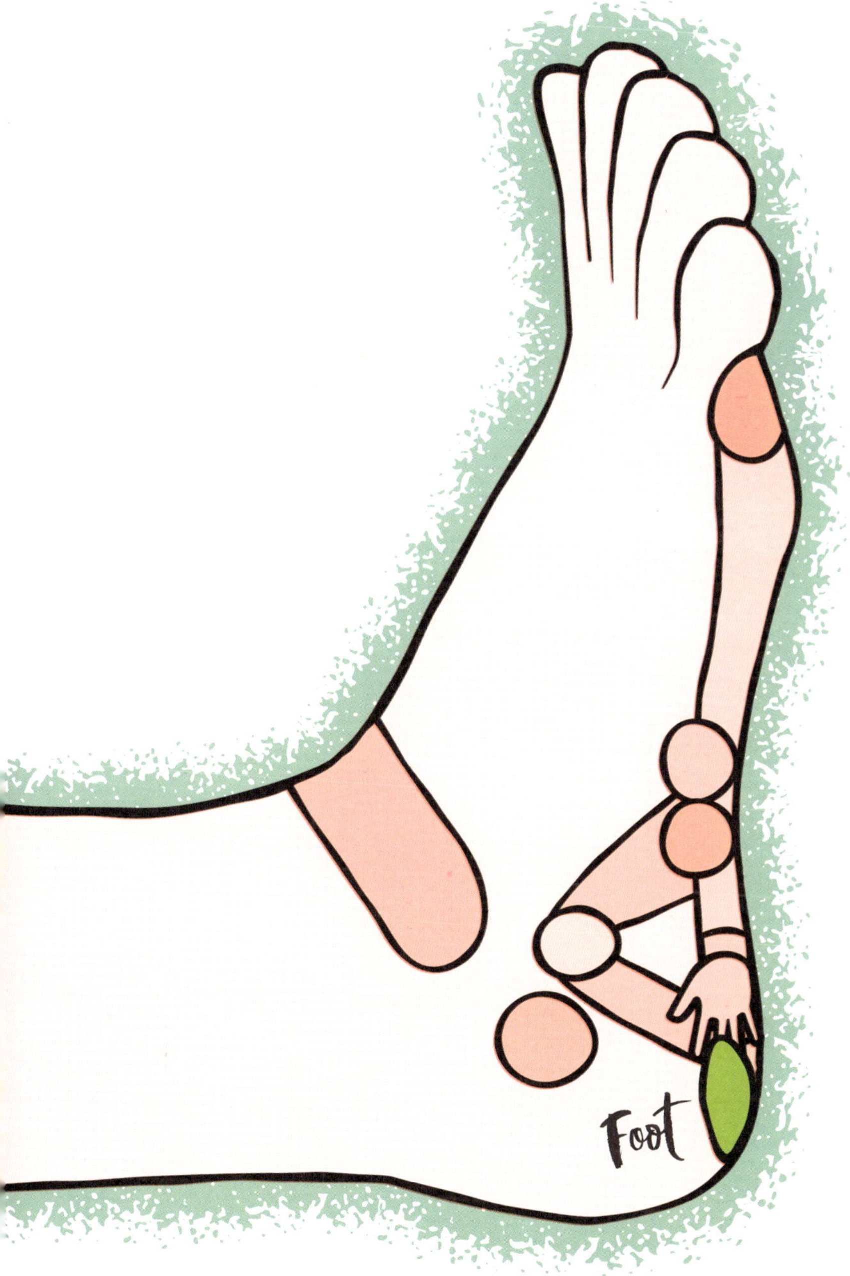

OUTER EDGE FOR ARMS AND LEGS

OVARIES / TESTES

The ovaries and the testes reflexes share the same reflex location. They are located on the outer heel of both feet, below and slightly behind the outer ankle bone.

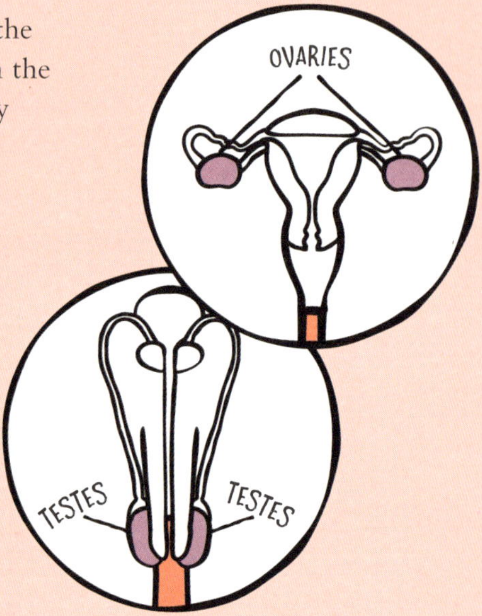

How to work the reflex

Begin by placing the pad of your thumb on the outer edge of the left foot, close to the end of the heel. Apply your thumb roll along the outer edge, reflexing the area below the outer ankle bone. Repeat several times. Continue reflexing the entire area of the outer heel, below the ankle bone, for some time to thoroughly work the ovaries/testes reflex. If you find a sensitive area, stop and hold it with the pad of your thumb for a minute or until tenderness eases. While holding, you can apply slow, circular movements with your thumb. After you have completed the left foot, use the same techniques in the same area on the right foot.

TIP: USE LIGHT PRESSURE

When you are working close below the ankle bone, explore the area with light pressure as it can be very sensitive.

Benefits of working the reflex

The ovaries reflex on the feet corresponds to the ovaries in the female body. The ovaries produce and release eggs into the female reproductive tract and produce the hormones estrogen and progesterone. Working the ovaries reflex can assist in menstrual health and may improve fertility.

The testes reflex on the feet corresponds to the testes in the male body. The testes, also called testicles, are oval-shaped organs that make and store sperm and produce the hormone testosterone. Working the testes reflex may improve fertility.

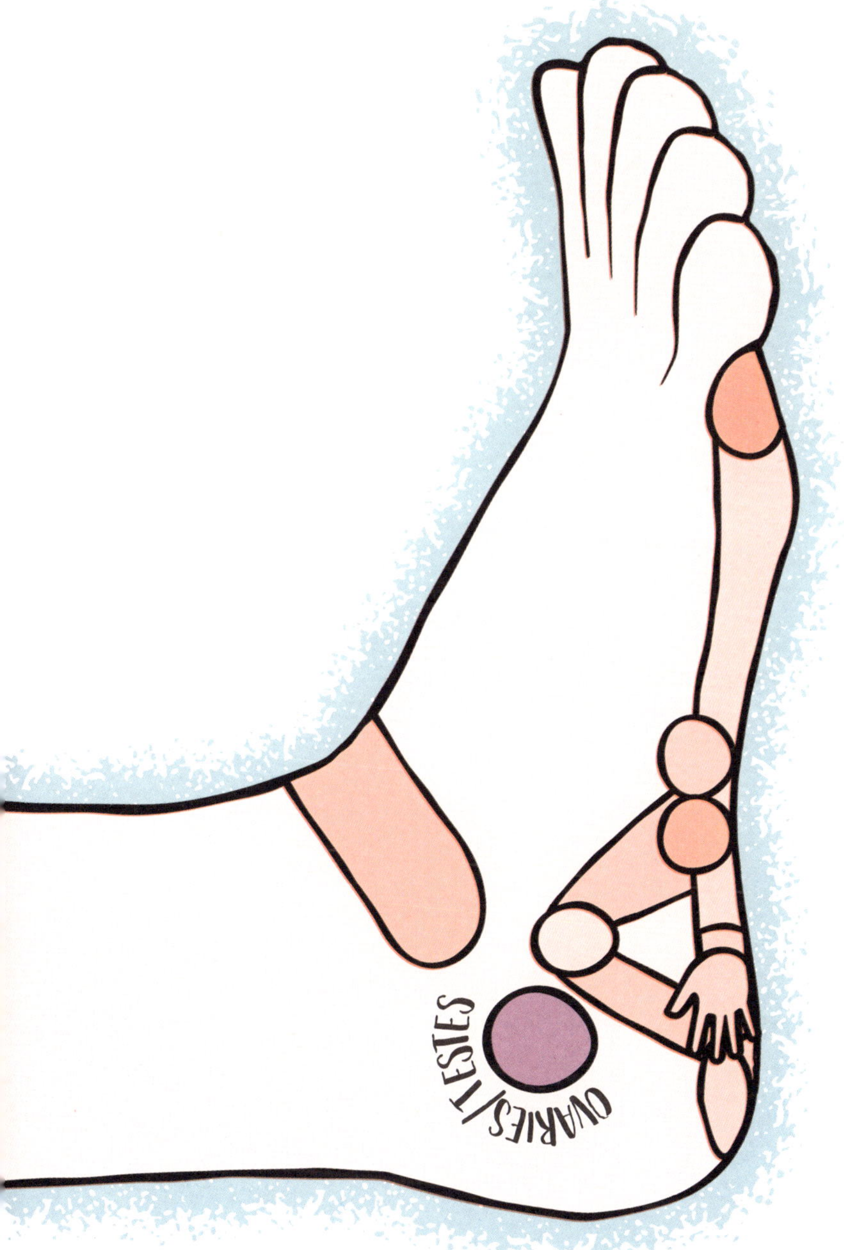

OUTER EDGE FOR ARMS AND LEGS

Ailment directory

Reflexology can be beneficial for a wide variety of health issues, easing pain and discomfort as well as helping to reduce or eliminate other symptoms. Each ailment in this alphabetically organized list is followed by the reflex points you can work for relief. All reflex points are listed in order of priority.

ADRENAL FATIGUE
- *Adrenal gland reflex p74*
- *Pituitary gland reflex p30*

Prolonged stress can cause the adrenal glands to fatigue and cause a variety of symptoms from tiredness and feeling down to weight gain.

ALLERGIES
- *Liver reflex p68*
- *Sinus reflex p34*

The liver cleanses the blood from toxins and chemical buildup, which may contribute to allergies.

ANXIETY
- *Diaphragm reflex p60*
- *Solar plexus reflex p62*
- *Adrenal gland reflex p74*
- *Pituitary gland reflex p30*

Relaxing the diaphragm muscle can help us to breathe more easily.

ARTHRITIS
- *Corresponding body reflexes*
- *Liver reflex p68*
- *Adrenal gland reflex p74*

For pain and stiffness associated with arthritis, first work the reflexes that correspond to the affected body part.

ASTHMA
- *Lung reflex p52*
- *Adrenal gland reflex p74*

It is important to help the lungs and bronchial tubes to relax, which may help ease laboured breathing.

BRONCHITIS
- *Lung reflex p52*
- *Adrenal gland reflex p74*

Bronchitis symptoms include a cough, chest discomfort and shortness of breath.

BURSITIS (SHOULDER, ELBOW OR KNEE)
- *Corresponding body reflexes*
- *Adrenal gland reflex p74*

Bursitis is an inflammation of the fluid-filled sac in knee, elbow or shoulder joints.

CROHN'S DISEASE
- *Small intestine reflex p80*
- *Colon reflex p82*
- *Adrenal gland reflex p74*

Crohn's disease is an inflammatory bowel disease, which can affect different areas of the digestive tract.

COLD/FLU
- *Head reflexes p28–45*
- *Chest reflex p20*
- *Upper and mid abdominal reflexes p20*
- *Thymus gland reflex p56*

Helping the immune system to work more efficiently is key to getting over a cold or flu faster.

CONSTIPATION
- *Stomach reflex p64*
- *Small intestine reflex p80*
- *Colon reflex p82*
- *Gallbladder reflex p70*
- *Liver reflex p68*

Constipation often means that the digestive tract is not working efficiently.

DEPRESSION
- *All of both feet p116–121*
- *Brain reflex p28*
- *Pituitary gland reflex p30*

A relaxing and soothing reflexology routine on both feet can help a person feel better overall.

DERMATITIS (ECZEMA/ ATOPIC DERMATITIS)
- *Corresponding body reflexes*
- *Liver reflex p68*
- *Adrenal gland reflex p74*

For symptoms of itching, redness and dry skin, begin with working the reflexes corresponding to the affected body part.

DIABETES

- *Pancreas reflex p72*

In some forms of diabetes, the pancreas is not producing enough insulin, which is responsible for decreasing blood sugar (glucose).

DIARRHOEA

- *Small intestine reflex p80*
- *Colon reflex p82*

When experiencing the discomforts of diarrhoea, work the colon reflexes.

DIVERTICULITIS

- *Colon reflex p82*
- *Adrenal gland reflex p74*

Diverticulitis is an inflammatory disease, which can affect the sigmoid colon, with symptoms such as pain, nausea and disturbance of bowel function.

DIZZINESS

- *Ear reflex p44*
- *Occiput reflex p32*

Dizziness is often caused by an imbalance of the inner ear.

EAR INFECTION

- *Ear reflex p44*
- *Thymus gland reflex p56*

Ear infections can be very painful.

ELBOW PAIN AND TENNIS ELBOW (EPICONDYLITIS)

- *Elbow reflex p110*
- *Arm reflex p108*
- *Adrenal gland reflex p74*

Epicondylitis can be caused by irritation of the tissue connecting forearm muscle to the elbow.

EYE FATIGUE

- *Eye reflex p42*
- *Occiput reflex p32*

One of the most common causes of eye fatigue is staring too long at digital devices.

GASTRITIS

- *Stomach reflex p64*
- *Adrenal gland reflex p74*

Gastritis is an inflammation of the stomach lining.

GALLSTONE

- *Gallbladder reflex p70*
- *Liver reflex p68*

The gallbladder plays an important role in regulating cholesterol which, when hardened, can form the most common gallstones.

HEADACHE

- *Head reflexes p28–45*
- *Occiput reflex p32*
- *Neck/cervical spine reflex p94*

Headache pain can have a variety of causes and can be felt in different areas of your head.

HEARTBURN (ACID REFLUX)

- *Solar plexus reflex p62*
- *Diaphragm reflex p60*
- *Stomach reflex p64*
- *Neck/cervical spine reflex p94*
- *Oesophagus reflex p54*

When suffering from acid reflux, you might feel discomfort in the chest when acid travels up from the stomach through the oesophagus.

HIATAL HERNIA

- *Lower part of oesophagus reflex p54*
- *Diaphragm reflex p60*
- *Stomach reflex p64*

Hiatal hernia is caused by part of the stomach bulging through the diaphragm muscle.

HICCUPS
• *Diaphragm reflex p60*
• *Neck/cervical spine reflex p94*
• *Chest reflex p20*
Hiccups are sudden spasms of the diaphragm muscle.

HIGH BLOOD PRESSURE (HYPERTENSION)
• *Heart reflex p50*
• *Solar plexus reflex p62*
It is important to relax the entire body of a person who experiences high blood pressure.

HIP PAIN
• *Hip reflex p114*
For any hip pain, work the broader area on and around the hip reflex.

INGUINAL HERNIA
• *Small intestine reflex p80*
Inguinal hernia can cause severe pain from the intestine bulging through a weakened abdominal wall.

IRRITABLE BOWEL SYNDROME (IBS)
• *Stomach reflex p64*
• *Small intestine reflex p80*
• *Colon reflex p82*
IBS is an intestinal disorder, with symptoms such as nausea, bloating, abdominal cramping, diarrhoea and constipation.

JAW TENSION
• *Jaw reflex p38*
TMJ can cause pain in the jaw joint and muscles.

KIDNEY STONE
• *Kidney reflex p76*
• *Ureter reflex p78*
• *Urinary bladder reflex p92*
Kidney stones are small, hard mineral deposits of mineral and acid salts inside your kidneys.

KNEE PAIN
• *Knee reflex p118*
• *Adrenal gland reflex p74*
For knee pain, work foremost on and around the knee reflex on the same side as your affected knee.

LEG PAIN AND LEG CRAMPS
• *Leg reflex p116*
If you experience pain from too much vigorous exercise, leg cramps or other causes of leg pain, reflex the entire triangular area of the leg reflex.

LOWER BACK PAIN AND STIFFNESS (LUMBAGO)
• *Lumbar spine reflex p98*
• *Sacrum reflex p100*
• *Pelvic reflex p20*
• *Adrenal gland reflex p74*
For lower back pain and stiffness, it is helpful to relax the muscles attached to the lumbar spine in addition to relaxing the broader lumbar area.

MIGRAINE
• *Brain reflexes p28*
• *Head reflexes p28–45*
• *Neck/cervical spine reflex p94*
• *Occiput reflex p32*
When suffering from migraines, reflex the entire bottom of both big toes.

MORNING SICKNESS
• *Solar plexus reflex p62 (see Contraindications and precautions, first trimester pregnancy, p10)*
Many women suffer from nausea in the first trimester of pregnancy.

NAUSEA
• *Stomach reflex p64*
• *Solar plexus reflex p62*
• *Diaphragm reflex p60*
Nausea of any kind can be helped by first holding the stomach and solar plexus reflexes on the soft sole of both feet for a while.

NECK PAIN AND STIFF NECK
• *Neck/cervical spine reflex p94*
• *Occiput reflex p32*
• *Shoulder reflex p46*
To ease neck tension, pain and stiffness it is helpful to work the lower half and inner edge of the big toe.

PRE-MENSTRUAL SYNDROME (PMS) AND MENSTRUAL CRAMPS

- *Uterus reflex p104*
- *Ovary reflex p122*
- *Pituitary gland reflex p30*

Premenstrual Syndrome or PMS usually starts about one week before menstruation.

PROSTATE ISSUES/ ENLARGED PROSTATE

- *Prostate reflex p104*
- *Adrenal gland reflex p74*

Many men, as they age, have an enlarged prostate, which affects normal urination.

PSORIASIS

- *Corresponding body reflexes*
- *Adrenal gland reflex p74*
- *Liver reflex p68*

Psoriasis, a chronic skin disorder, can cause itchy, red, raised, scaly patches to appear on the skin.

SCIATICA

- *Sciatic nerve reflex p84*
- *Lower back reflex p98*
- *Leg reflex p116*
- *Adrenal gland reflex p74*

The sciatic nerve starts at the lower back and runs through the buttock and down each leg.

SHOULDER PAIN

- *Shoulder reflex p46*
- *Shoulder blade reflex p48*
- *Upper back/thoracic spine reflex p96*
- *Adrenal gland reflex p74*

Shoulder pain can be caused by a variety of issues from injury, muscle tension, to arthritis and more.

SINUS CONGESTION AND SINUSITIS

- *Sinus reflex p34*
- *Adrenal gland reflex p74*

From allergies to cold, you can find great relief from sinus congestion by working the bottom and sides of all toes.

SORE THROAT AND TONSILLITIS

- *Head reflexes p28–45*
- *Neck/cervical spine reflex p94*
- *Thymus gland reflex p56*
- *Adrenal gland reflex p74*

A sore throat is often the first sign of a cold, whereas tonsillitis is an inflammation or infection of the tonsils at the back of the throat.

STOMACH ACHE

- *Stomach reflex p64*
- *Diaphragm reflex p60*
- *Solar plexus reflex p62*

Stomach pain can be caused by a variety of issues.

THYROID DYSFUNCTION

- *Thyroid reflex p40*
- *Pituitary gland reflex p30*

The thyroid gland in the base of the neck is essential for producing hormones that affect metabolism. Over- or under-function of the thyroid gland is a common problem.

TINNITUS

- *Ear reflex p44*
- *Neck/cervical spine reflex p94*
- *Occiput reflex p32*

Tinnitus is commonly referred to as ringing or buzzing in the ears, and can be temporary or chronic.

TOOTHACHE

- *Teeth reflex p36*
- *Jaw reflex p38*

If the cause of the toothache is unknown, make sure to see a dentist.

ULCER

- *Stomach reflex p64*
- *Small intestine reflex p80*

Common symptoms of stomach ulcers are burning stomach pain, bloating, feeling of fullness, fatty food intolerance and nausea.

URINARY TRACT INFECTION (UTI)

- *Urinary bladder reflex p92*
- *Ureter reflex p78*
- *Kidney reflex p76*

The burning of a urinary tract infection can be very painful.

Illustrations are in italics

ACKNOWLEDGEMENTS

A special thank you to my husband Steven for your love and support and for believing in my work. Thank you to my dear friend Kathy Ann Reynolds for your friendship, love and countless hours of editing; my teacher, mentor and friend Bill Flocco for your knowledge, wisdom and ongoing support; Lisa Chan for your friendship, love and teachings of reflexology and life; Rosemarie Sabounchian for proofreading and supporting me in so many ways; my family and friends for your support and patience; my clients for allowing me to work with you; my students, who are also my greatest teachers; my friends of the World Reflexology Foundation, Reflexology Associations in the US, Europe and around the world, who keep inspiring me every day; and a fantastic team of editors at Quarto Publishing. I am deeply grateful to be able to share my passion and knowledge of reflexology.